YOU vs YOU

❖❖❖❖

Sports Psychology
For Life

You vs. You: Sports Psychology for Life

Mazz Marketing, Inc.

© 2005

Wayne Mazzoni

Thank You...

I would like to thank several people for helping make this book a reality. To my wife Keli who deserves a lifetime award for putting up with me. My sons Colby and Brayden who keep my life in perspective. Ken Samuelson whose editing work helped make my ideas understandable. To Deb Nozzolillo for her graphic design, professionalism, and attention to detail. Thanks to Karl Ravech for being kind enough to write the forward. To the great Dave Matthews for music which inspires every cell within me. To my Dad for listening to all of my crazy ideas. Finally, to all the players who I have had the privilege to coach.

In November of 1998 at the age of 33 I suffered a heart attack. I was hardly the first young man to be dealt such a hand and I will certainly not be the last. How I and others respond to such challenges is what this book is all about. Over the course of a lifetime we all will encounter forks in the road. Simplifying things, we can either choose the easy path or the one that involves work, commitment and dedication. The latter is the more rewarding and it is also the more difficult. Since my heart attack, I have chosen the path of most resistance not least. I also have discovered that along the way I've needed an occasional nudge to keep going. Nobody can navigate through life alone yet often times we feel as if it is us against the world. Whether you are trying to earn a degree in school, the respect of your peers or a spot on a Major League Baseball team, dreams are what motivate us every day. I encourage you to dream big, to accept the mole hills that will rise along the way and to squash them before they become mountains. You control your own destiny, take responsibility for your actions, be accountable for the outcomes and enjoy the journey. I am now 39 years old and feel better than I have at any other point in my life.

- Karl Ravech, Anchor, ESPN

CONTENTS

"Nothing in the world can take the place of persistence. Talent will not; Nothing is more common than unsuccessful people with talent. Genius will not; Unrewarded genius is almost legendary; Education will not; The world is full of educated derelicts. Persistence and determination alone are omnipotent. The slogan "press on" has solved and always will solve the problems of the human race."

- Calvin Coolidge

INTRODUCTION

"There is nothing noble in being superior to some other man. The true nobility is in being superior to your previous self."
- Hindustani proverb

We all have dreams. When we lay our head down on the pillow at night, we dream of all the things we would like to achieve and accomplish in our lives.

However, we often find that staying on track can be difficult. If we are fortunate enough, we have a friend, partner, or coach who may help to keep us focused. Nevertheless, at some point it becomes evident that true motivation comes from within.

The impetus for this book has come from my coaching career where I have often seen my role as not just a teacher of sports, but also as a teacher of life. Sports, after all, parallels life - in both cases the real success is in the effort. If the end goals are achieved, that's great. But, no matter what the outcome, if you can truly say "I did my best" - you are a real winner. I hope that in some way this book will be of help. I wish you well.

- Wayne Mazzoni

1.
You Are Not Going To Be Perfect

*"Perfection does not exist. To understand it is the triumph
of human intelligence; to desire to possess it is the most
dangerous kind of madness."*
- Alfred de Musset

While much of what will be discussed in this book is about how to keep yourself motivated and performing at your best, it is certainly not about achieving perfection. Attempting to do things perfectly is the important thing. Whether it's during a practice or a game, striving for perfection is of the utmost importance, though hard to achieve. A pitcher in a baseball game may pitch great, but he will still give up walks and hits. There have only been 16 perfect games (no walks, hits, or errors) in Major League Baseball history. Field goals go wide, free throws hit the rim, putts lip out. No matter how hard you try you will seldom reach perfection. It is important to know this going in to any endeavor, so that when you come up short at times, you will not be completely defeated. It is impossible to be perfect in any area of life, expecting so will only set you up for defeat. Again, it is the journey towards peak performance that really matters.

The same thing happens in life. You clean a house, your kids make a mess. You wash your car, then it rains. Life happens - life is not perfect. Get used to it now. When you expect all things in your life to go perfectly according to plan, you are setting yourself up for trouble. If you are excited to go to a game, a party, or a job interview, and you expect the ride to be traffic free, you are setting yourself up for trouble. Life is not perfect. Accidents happen. Roads need repairing. Congestion builds. Of course, all of us hope we don't have a hassle, but if you find traffic, the way you deal with it is crucial. You can let it drive you nuts or accept it and learn that next time you will leave much earlier, have a backup route planned, and bring a cell phone to call and let others know you will be late. When you expect things to go smoothly, you often set yourself up for trouble.

2.

You Can Control Your Attitude

"I am an optimist.
It does not seem too much use being anything else."
- Winston Churchill

"What one approves, another scorns, and thus his nature each discloses;
You find the rosebush full of thorns, I find the thornbush full of roses."
- Arthur Guiterman

"The pessimist sees difficulty in every opportunity.
The optimist sees the opportunity in every difficulty."
- Winston Churchill

There will be many situations over the course of your life and athletic career where circumstances will be out of your control. You cannot control your coaches, teammates, umpires, referees, judges, or your opponent. What you can control is your attitude toward them. There will be times when you throw the perfect pass that is dropped. You certainly can't control a receiver, but you can control your ability to react to his mistake. You can yell and scream and make him nervous about the next one or you can pat him on the back and build his confidence. There will be many opportunities along the way where you will be faced with a choice of how to react. Becoming a mature person and athlete means that you will choose the reaction that is best for you and for your team. Your attitude towards all aspects of your life is in your control. Your attitude towards those in charge, to those you view below you, to women, or men, or minorities, to foreigners, to animals is in your control. When you take the time to look deeply, you will find that you have attitudes about so many things in life. Many of our viewpoints come from our parents or the environment in which we were raised. You might think that all boys with long hair are drug addicts, until you meet a kid with long hair and find out that he is just like you. The more you can change your attitude and treat all people the same and with respect, the better off you will be. Often, what we don't like in others is what we don't like in ourselves.

3.

It's About the Challenge

"The rung of a ladder was never meant to rest upon,
but only to hold a man's foot long enough to enable him
to put the other somewhat higher."
- Thomas Henry Huxley

"It's not the size of the dog in the fight,
but the size of the fight in the dog."
- Archie Griffin

Without a challenge, sports are hardly worth playing. We don't always need a challenge in life as much as we do in sports. For example, you might meet the person of your dreams and while you would accept having to work to win their affection, it would be just fine if they loved you without having to work so hard. Given a choice most of us would rather meet and date someone without having to beat out ten other people to win their affection. The same is true for our career. While we certainly will face challenges in our work, wouldn't it be great if you found the right job, company, and pay without having to work as hard?

Yet in sports, without challenge, we have nothing. If you play tennis but your opponent is terrible, you don't have a game. If you play softball and beat the other team by 40 runs, you don't have a game. This is why most people love golf since the game is played against yourself. If you play a very easy course, you might not like the challenge. In golf, you are playing yourself, but the course as well. It gets even better when you play with friends and create games. The pressure and challenge of playing in high school or college, trying to make the professional tour and then to win once there, get even greater.

Sometimes we feel that if we had it easier, it would be better, but that is not really the case. To improve, to get playing time, to become a starter, to create a good work ethic, to win, to achieve is much sweeter when it is hard fought and earned.

4.

Team Work

"It is one of the most beautiful compensations of this life that no man can sincerely try to help another without helping himself."
- Ralph Waldo Emerson

"In union there is strength."
- Aesop

"United we stand, divided we fall."
- George Pope Morris

"Many hands make light work."
- John Heywood

A team is as only as strong as its weakest link. If the whole team knows a particular play, but one person does not, that person will ruin the play and maybe the game or even the season. In the military, the weakest link can cause lives.

Team sports are really individual sports played within a team concept. Being a team player does not mean that you shouldn't be concerned with your performance or role on the team. We all want to do the best we can. I doubt many people would rather be a bench warmer on a great team then a starter on a poor team. We all love to play. However, being a team player means that you will do all you can to help others be the best they can. No goals can be achieved completely alone and thus you need your teammates to be the best they can be if you hope to be the best you can. Being a true teammate means looking out for your follow teammates. This could be teaching them a certain technique or maybe a play they cannot seem to learn. It can also be helping them in other areas of their life away from athletics.

Being a good teammate means that you will encourage your teammates to do well, even if you are not having the best of days. You might strikeout with the bases loaded. This does not mean that you have to go into a corner and sulk. A true teammate would root for the next person up to get a hit. There will be times when a teammate needs you to come through just as you often need them to do the same. If there's no wind, row.

5.

Process, Not Outcome

*"The world cares very little about what a man or woman knows;
it is what the man or woman is able to do that counts."*
- Booker T. Washington

It is understandable that most of us get caught up in the outcome of our performance. After all we grow up watching professional sports, where players are judged by their statistics and teams by wins. While these things are certainly important and are often a good source of feedback as to how hard we are working, they do you little good when actually performing. If you are at the plate concerned only about getting a hit, shooting a free throw only hoping it goes in, or hitting a nine iron only with the goal of getting it close to the hole, you may find that when you focus only on the outcome you often miss it. Instead try focusing more on your state of mind and the process it takes to get the desired outcome. For example, you may want to think about just staying relaxed and seeing the ball. Maybe you should concentrate on just swinging easily. Whatever makes sense for your sport or skill. Try putting less focus on the outcome and more on what it will take to get that outcome.

6.
Change One Thing

"We cannot do everything at once,
but we can do something at once."
- Calvin Coolidge

So often we get wrapped up in trying to change everything that might need work in our game, all at once. You cannot rebuild all parts of your game in one day or at one time. You cannot lose weight all at once. You cannot build strength in a week. It takes patience and persistence. The best way to make lasting change is to take it in small steps. If you want to lose weight, it is not possible to go from eating poorly and not exercising, to eating perfectly with daily two hour workouts overnight. Make one change until it becomes a habit. It might simply be to eat whole wheat toast and egg whites in the morning, instead of pancakes, sausages, and biscuits. Once you have that change in place, try to make another which is in line with your long term goal of losing weight, or whatever else you have set for yourself.

This is a good skill to carry over to other parts of your life as well. If you are feeling stress coming from various sources in your life, try to take one area and begin to calm down. Maybe you drive to work in the morning in a complete rush, drinking coffee, eating a bagel, and listening to the news. All the while you are navigating the other cars and the road. By trying to drive in much slower, with the radio off, or peaceful music on, might be just the thing you need to get your day started off on the right foot.

Again, try to break any problem down into small steps and then take one of those steps with commitment until it becomes a way of life. Never forget that often you are one change away from going from bad to good, good to better, better to best. It might be a technical change, a strategic change, a growth of experience, or an attitude adjustment that turns your entire career around. That alone should keep you working your hardest at all times.

7.
Focus On The Very Good and Very Bad

"Everyone is trying to accomplish something big,
not realizing that life is made up of little things."
- Frank A. Clark

"Big jobs usually go to the men who prove their
ability to outgrow small ones."
- Ralph Waldo Emerson

Most of us spend our practice time focusing simply on random parts of all the skills we need to work on. Most of us have coaches that set practice plans for the team, but this still may not cover all the skills we need to work on. Coaches do care about the individual player, but the team is the first concern. You must be responsible for your own improvement and development outside of the team concept.

While it certainly makes sense to work on all phases of the abilities you need to perform your sport, I have found that working on what you do very well and very poorly makes a great deal of sense.

First, the good. Working on your best attributes builds confidence. It is usually fun, since you are good at it. Chances are this is your most valuable skill and the one that your team or your game needs the most. At the same time, you should also work very hard on the part(s) of your skills that are the weakest. Most of us don't like doing what we are not very good at. By making the extra effort to improve in this area, we learn what it feels like to overcome. Further, we turn into better players.

If you play first base for your softball team and are a great hitter, of course you will want to practice hitting as much as possible. But if scooping balls out of the dirt is your weakest part, this should be of major focus as well. There will be many times you team needs you to make those plays, regardless of how good you are at other parts of your game.

8.

You Can't Cram

*"God gives every bird its food, but He does
not throw it into the nest."*
-J.G. Holland

"If the power to do hard work is not a skill,
it's the best possible substitute for it."
- James A. Garfield

"For me, winning isn't something that happens suddenly
on the field when the whistle blows and the crowds roar.
Winning is something that builds physically and mentally
every day that you train and every night that you dream."
- Emmitt Smith

We have all been in school and crammed for a test. While it is not the best way to learn, we can do much better on a test by focusing all our effort just before we take it. This is not the same in other areas of life. You can't cram your garden. If you don't plant your vegetables at the right time, give them soil, sun, and water to grow, they won't. If harvest time is August, you can't put them in on July 31. You can cram for certain jobs at work. Not so for athletics.

Can you imagine running the New York City marathon in November, but not starting your training until a week before the race? Can you cram in all your running? Of course you can't. Learning the skills and the plays, learning the game, takes time and practice. It takes persistence. It should be fun, but it requires a consistent effort. The skills you learn build and allow for others. Teams take time to come together as a unit. Many of you who are reading this are in school and know all about cramming. Just know that this is not a skill that translates to athletics.

9.

Leadership

"No man is fit to command another that cannot command himself."
- William Penn

"I am more afraid of an army of 100 sheep led by a lion than an army of 100 lions led by a sheep."
- Talleyrand

"If you think you're too small to make a difference, you haven't been in bed with a mosquito."
- Anita Roddick

"Leadership: the art of getting someone else to do something you want done because he wants to do it."
- Dwight D. Eisenhower

Leadership is hard to define, but easy to see. Leaders do several things. Most importantly they lead themselves. To be a leader, your own life must be in order. Your studies, your family, your relationship, your athletic skills, must all be in line to be a leader. If you are constantly having problems in one or more areas of your life it is hard to lead. By the same token, it is truly hard to be a leader if you are not a good performer. You don't have to be the best player on the team, but you certainly need to be a key player. Leaders impact their teams in several ways.

First, their work ethic in both practice and games shows the rest of the team what they expect of themselves and thus others. It is hard to ask for extra effort of others, if one is not giving it themselves. In addition, leaders are capable of leading the team in good times and bad. When practice is going well, or the game is in hand, or the team is on a winning streak, leaders are important because they keep the team focused on the goal of continuing the streak as opposed to just enjoying what has already been done.

More importantly, leaders are needed when things are not going well. When practice is not running smoothly, the team is facing adversity in a game or season is when leadership is truly important. If the leaders of the team are beaten, then so is the team.

Most people underestimate the power of what one person can do. Leadership can set the course of the team by expecting more from the team then would otherwise be expected. Coaches can lead, but their impact can only go so far. When a player leads, it is even more persuading.

Another key quality of a leader is that they focus entirely on the current task at hand. While they take pride in previous accomplishments, they are more concerned with the challenge now. Instead of being concerned with future issues, they focus on the present moment and what needs to be done now.

Be aware that leading is much like coaching. One of the key rules of being a good coach is that players need to be coached differently. That is, one style does not work to motivate all people. Your job as a leader is to find the right tone to get the most out of others. For some that might be a challenging tone, for others a calming talk. To lift others up, you must be on higher ground.

10.

Persistence

Lincoln's Road to the White House: Failed in business in 1831. Defeated for Legislature in 1832. Second failure in business in 1833. Suffered nervous breakdown in 1836. Defeated for Speaker in 1838. Defeated for Elector in 1840. Defeated for Congress in 1843 & 1848. Defeated for Senate in 1855. Defeated for Vice President in 1856. Defeated for Senate in 1858. Elected President in 1860.

After Fred Astaire's first screen test, a 1933 memo from the MGM testing director said, "Can't act. Slightly bald. Can dance a little."

A relatively unsuccessful marketer of restaurant equipment, Ray Kroc didn't sell his first hamburger until age 52. At a time when many prepare for retirement, Kroc built McDonald's.

Walt Disney was fired by a newspaper for lacking ideas.

"Success seems to be largely a matter of hanging on after others have let go."
- William Feather

Above all else, winners show persistence. Persistence is the quality that will carry over from athletics to "real" life, more then any other. Persistence is simply that no matter what your place on the team, your skill level, your performance, your results, you are always trying to better yourself. It is constant and never ending improvement. You get cut from the team, you don't quit, but practice, improve and make it the next year. You get pulled from a game for playing badly, you learn from your mistakes and better yourself. You play a great game, but you still don't rest. Rather you are motivated to work even harder. The Japanese call this Kaizen--the business practice of orderly, constant, and continuous improvement.

This quality is inherent in all of us. After all humans have grown, improved, and survived. We are constantly improving our quality of life, albeit with set backs, in many areas. When it's applied to athletics, persistence is more then just surviving, it is constantly seeking ways to improve yourself. It is the quality that should be there above all the others.

11.

Opportunity

"Opportunity is missed by most people because it is dressed in overalls and looks like work."
- Thomas Edison

"I find that the harder I work, the more luck I seem to have."
- Thomas Jefferson

"Two shoe salesmen...find themselves in a rustic backward part of Africa. The first salesman wires back to his head office: "There is no prospect of sales. Natives do not wear shoes!' The other sales man wires: 'No one wears shoes here. We can dominate the market. Send all possible stock.'"
- Akio Morita

Is opportunity something that is given to you or is it something that you earn? Winners create opportunities for themselves by always being prepared so that when the time comes, they are ready for the challenge. If a reserve player stays out all night because he doesn't think he will get in the game, when that chance comes it will be hard to take advantage of it. Opportunity is made, it is created, it is not given. Often those who don't get the opportunity are quick to make excuses or pass the blame to others. If they are not getting the amount of playing time they feel is deserved, they may blame the coach instead of really looking at what they need to do to be a better player.

There is certainly some luck that plays into our lives, but luck seems to come to those that have worked hard. By working hard, you are often in the right position to take advantage of a break when it happens. If you are an actor in an Off-Broadway play who gets discovered by a movie producer who was at the show to see another actor, is that really luck? I would not call it luck, when the person first decided to go into acting as opposed to a career that had immediate pay and job security. I also don't consider it luck since they must be a talented actor if a professional producer liked their skills. It may be a little lucky that the producer happened to be there that particular night, but chances are a very talented actor was going to be discovered sooner or later.

It will always come back to haunt you when you think you are owed an opportunity. Many players often think that they are owed an opportunity when the person in front of them is hurt, or leaves the team, or graduates, or signs with another team. But that is not the case. The job of a coach or general manager is to give his or her team the best chance to win. If that means brining up a person from a team below, bringing in a new player, shifting the position of someone else, that is what they will do. It is your job to be the best you can be and the coach's job to do what they think is best. I hear, all too often, of what players and parents feel about their coaches. It seems to me that there are way to many excuses, such as "the coach has favorite players," "there are politics involved," "the coach doesn't know what he or she is doing." The next time you are likely to use this as an excuse, remember that most coaches are in coaching since they like to teach and help others. If not, they would most likely be in a different, higher paying career. Take responsibility for your opportunities and you will soon find that you have a great deal more of them. If opportunity doesn't knock, build a door.

12.
Adversity

"Adversity introduces a man to himself."
- Anonymous

*"One of the secrets of life is to make stepping stones
out of stumbling blocks."*
- Jack Penn

"No pressure, no diamonds."
- Mary Case

It has been said that the road to success is always under construction. There will be many obstacles on your path to success--injuries, playing time, officials, coaches, teammates, etc. Quite simply, life is not fair. Often you can do exactly as you intended and not get the result you want. You can throw the perfect pitch which should be a double play ground ball, yet it turns into an error instead. The kick returned for a touchdown is called back due to a penalty. A key player is lost due to injury. The field conditions are poor. A big lead is blown. No season is going to be without adversity. How each player and the team reacts to these inevitable challenges will determine how well they do. Seasons are like roller coasters. There are always ups and downs. Be the one who shows the way when things get tough. Be the one who wants the ball when others don't. If you make a mistake, don't hide the rest of the game. Get ready for the next play and hope it comes your way.

13.
No Overnight Sensations

*"The vision of a champion is someone who is bent over,
drenched in sweat, at the point of exhaustion when
no one else is watching."*
- Anson Dorrance

"If at first you don't succeed, you're running about average"
- M.H. Alderson

"It takes twenty years to become an overnight success."
- Eddie Cantor

In sports, in business, in life, there are very few overnight sensations. Although you may have never heard of them until they get the chance to shine, the majority of the work was done long before. Take a backup quarterback. He may sit and watch for many games or even years, but at some point he will get his chance. If he turns out to play great and become a star, chances are it was not due to the fact that he just became good when he got on the field. He spent years working on his technique, working out, studying film, knowing the plays.

All the work was done well before he finally got the chance to shine. If he waited to get motivated only after opportunity to came, he certainly would not have done as well.

To become adept at anything in life, it needs to be practiced often. Nothing worth attaining ever really comes easy, especially in the world of sports. Think of Olympic athletes who spend four years training for an event which can take only minutes to complete. Think of all the boxers and skaters and runners who burst onto the scene. The work they put into their careers before they became stars is what made them so.

14.
Expectations

"If you want a track team to win the high jump,
you find one person who can jump seven feet,
not seven people who can jump one foot."
- Louis Terman

"I don't know the key to success,
but the key to failure is to try and please everyone."
- Bill Cosby

Tom Landry once said, "Coaches get players to do what they're not willing to do so they become what they always wanted to be." That is certainly a great quote. However, you can't always count on having a coach who motivates you in this way. In fact, the more you are self-motivated as an athlete the better off you will be. Having your own expectations and goals is very important. Friends, teammates, parents, coaches, and the media will all have a view of what they expect out of you. Often the opinion of others may be geared too low or set too high. For this reason it is important to set your own goals so that you can measure your progress and performance.

Having expectations during game time can be a positive or negative. I have found that the best-prepared athletes on any given play are often those that expect the worst. For example, the receiver who expects the quarterback to make the perfect throw right on his numbers, often has a difficult time adjusting to a badly thrown ball. The receiver who has practiced catching all the toughest throws and who, at game time, expects the ball to be thrown poorly to him, will be prepared if and when it does. If the ball is thrown perfectly then it takes no adjustment. The same theory holds for the catcher who calls for the curve ball or the shortstop taking a double play feed from the second baseman. Expect and prepare for the worst and then be pleasantly surprised when the play works out just as it's supposed to.

15.
Input = Output

"I like to work half a day. I don't care if it's the first twelve hours or the second twelve hours. I just put in my half day every day."
- Kemmons Wilson

"The spirit, the will to win, and the will to excel are the things that endure. These qualities are so much more important than the events that occur."
- Vince Lombardi

"Hard work has made it easy. That is my secret. That is why I win."
- Nadia Comaneci

If your car gets 30 miles to the gallon and you have a ten gallon tank, you can drive about 300 miles. It's very simple. You get out what you put in. The same is true in most areas of our lives. If you have a relationship that you take for granted and don't put much time or effort into it, problems will occur. If you don't practice hard, work out hard, and give your all each contest, don't expect to win or be a great player. And if you are one of those fortunate enough to be much more talented then the others, you will find out that you can't expect to get by on talent alone. Michael Jordan, Tiger Woods, Roger Clemens, to name a few, have great skill, but they each worked hard to maintain their level of play. You don't get to the top level and then just coast - the competition is just too good. The harder you work in the weight room, on the practice court, in the pool, watching game film, the better you will be.

While politics, nepotism, and other factors, can enter your working life and give unfair advantages to those that may not deserve it, most often you will typically get back what you put in. If you put in hard work, you will eventually receive your due in terms of financial rewards, more responsibility, a promotion, etc. Life, of course, is not always fair and perfect, but in the long haul those that give will eventually receive.

16.
Giving All You Have Is Success

"The best way to appreciate leisure is to work for it."
- La Rochefoucauld

"You find that you have peace of mind and can enjoy yourself,
get more sleep, and rest when you know that it was a
one hundred percent effort that you gave - win or lose."
- Gordie Howe

After each day is over, each practice, each workout, each game, after a season is over or a career, what really determines your success is knowing you gave all that you have to give. If you lose, if you did not reach your goals, if things did not work out, but you gave all you had, you are a winner. You can look into the mirror and know you gave it your all. While so many have a goal of making it as a professional in their sport, the reality is that very few have the talent necessary to achieve this goal. For most of us, no matter how hard we try, we will not be able to make it to that level. Are you a failure if you did everything you could to take your career as far as possible, but it did not lead to your goal of playing as a pro? Of course you're not. What matters is that you gave it your all. Measure your wealth not by the things you have, but by the things you have for which you would not take money.

If you are not already, one day you may become a parent. While much of how your child develops is directly related to the care, attention, and love you give them, often other factors influence the type of people we all eventually become. If you do all you can to be a loving and caring parent, but your child turns out to be a criminal, for example, then you can rest knowing that you did what you could do. It does not mean you will be thrilled with their lifestyle and that you still do not make every attempt to help them, but at some point there is only so much one can do. If you have done all you could, that is success.

17.
Perfect Practice. Practice Hours.

"Nothing is particularly hard if you divide it into small jobs."
- Henry Ford

Earlier we discussed that it is unfair to expect perfect performance from ourselves. However, when we practice our skills, our goal should be to do them perfectly. If you don't practice the proper way, you can do more harm then good and are simply reinforcing a bad habit or poor technique. To do something better, the first key is to stop doing it incorrectly. The body learns by muscle memory, thus each time you do something wrong, it ingrains that wrong skill. Learning a new way to do something must be done just right, especially when you are trying to undo a bad habit. Don't make the mistake of thinking you can change years of doing something one way just because a coach told you. It takes perfect practice.

In addition, when you are practicing, either on your own or with a team, more important then how much time you put in, is what you put into that time. I have seen that at many of my various jobs. Many employees work a lot of hours, but they don't get nearly as much done as others who are in less. The amount of time one is at work is not as important as what one does when there.

A focused one hour is better then a lazy three. In fact, by taking more time but doing less, you are actually building in a habit of laziness. You are much better off working harder for shorter periods and using the additional time to rest or do other things. Remember, you get better or worse each day.

18.

Critic In The Mirror

"True success is overcoming the fear of being unsuccessful"
- Paul Sweeney

As the Michael Jackson song goes "I'm starting with the man in the mirror. I'm asking him to change his ways," so goes this nugget. There will be so many people who judge and comment on your ability, performance, effort, and so forth. While we are only human and care about what others might think, only we know what is real. Others may give you praise, but only you will know if you deserve it or not. Others may fault you, only you know if you don't deserve that as well. My advice is after each practice, each workout, each game is to find a mirror and look right into it. The feeling you get from inside will be enough to tell you the real answer. Did you give your best? If not, find out why and try to make changes and do better next time. If you did, feel the pride that comes from giving it your all.

19.

Start With The End In Mind

"You got to be careful if you don't know where you're going,
because you might not get there."
- Yogi Berra

Starting with the end in mind equates to having a long term goal. Whether your goal is individual or team oriented, it gives you direction in the steps along the way. Often as a coach I have to conduct early morning practices. Few players like getting up (and often finishing practice) before the sun comes up. Coaches don't love it either for that matter. So why do it? Well, certain times this is the only available hours to practice. We could just skip it and come back the next day, but this will get us no closer to our goal. If you knew that early practices would guarantee reaching your goal, they suddenly would not be so hard. While they don't guarantee anything, not doing them almost assures you of not getting there. For those of you have who achieved great goals, you know that the joy, the pride, and the honor are well worth the price that was paid to get them. If you can keep that achievement feeling in your mind, you will find the more day to day, seemingly mundane tasks much easier to do.

Whether your goals are team oriented, such as winning the Super Bowl, a conference championship, a game against a big rival, or individual such as becoming a starter, or winning a batting title, having the end in mind will keep you motivated to do what it takes to get there. When I thought about writing this book, I was motivated by the idea, but several times I tried to get started, but could not. I did not have a plan in mind, I simply had a slew of loose notes taken over the years. What really helped me was to design a cover for the book. Even though I am not a graphic artist by any stretch, I made up a make shift cover which helped guide me as I wrote. I then set out to try to finish one note a day on the book. This eventually became the book you are reading. When you look at any task as a whole piece it can seem too big, but if you can break it down into smaller pieces and have your end goal in mind, that will be of great help. If you are trying to lose weight, put your favorite picture of yourself on every spot in your house where you keep food. The end, losing weight and looking good, will keep you motivated along the way.

20.
Feedback, Not Failure

"We didn't lose the game; we just ran out of time."
- Vince Lombardi

*"A life spent making mistakes is not only more honorable,
but more useful than a life spent doing nothing."*
- George Bernard Shaw

"A man's errors are his portals of discovery."
- James Joyce

*"I am not judged by the number of times I fail, but by the number
of times I succeed; and the number of times I succeed is in direct
proportion to the number of times I can fail and keep on trying."*
- Tom Hopkins

There are two ways to fail. One is where it destroys your will to continue or compete. The other is where it builds your resolve so as to not repeat the experience. In the business world, if you start a company which fails, it is not a total failure if you learned along the way.

If you learned why it went out of business and how you would do it better the next time, then you are failing upward. It might lead you to a business venture down the road that turns out to be a success. Writers don't write a masterpiece the first time out. It is the same way in athletics. If you fail at achieving your goal, but learned why you failed, then you have the knowledge and motivation needed to succeed the next time. You might fall ten times, so just stand up eleven.

21.
Enough About The Weather

"The world is full of willing people; some willing to work, the rest willing to let them."
- Robert Frost

"The first man gets the oyster, the second man gets the shell."
- Andrew Carnegie

While some athletic competitions are conducted indoors, many take place in the natural elements. The more you concern yourself with the wind, rain, snow, or any type of extreme weather, you are defeated. When it is cold, everyone knows it's cold, so there's no need to keep bringing it up. The same goes for the heat. When cold, try to stay warm, when warm try to stay cool. The other team plays in the same temperature. If you don't like to pitch in the cold, I'm afraid you are not going to be able to pitch for the Red Sox in the World Series. Gets cold in Boston in October. Take the ball, go to the mound, get people out, keep quiet.

We lost because we had to drive far. Our pregame meal wasn't good. There was traffic on the way to the game. This other team is really good. That quarterback is good. What is the pitcher's record? Is this team good? STOP. Go out and play. Do your best. Whether they are 30 and 0 or 0 and 30, play the same, try to win. Keep playing and trying to win every game, and let someone tell you when the season is over. No need to try and figure out the playoff scenarios, just keep trying to win every time you compete.

22.
Small Gap Between Good and Great

"If you can't change facts, try bending your attitude."
- George Eliot

The best example of the small gap between good and great comes from a comedy routine from Jerry Seinfeld about Olympic sprinters. He jokes about how the first guy across the line is the best in the world, the guy two inches behind him, no one has ever heard of. How true. In so many sports the difference between winning and losing is so small, just as the difference between being good and great. Two athletes can be similar in so many ways, but one exceeds the performance of the other by a much greater difference. Often the key to this difference is the attention to detail. Once one possesses the basic skills of a particular sport, the one who becomes a professional in terms of their commitment to learning all the aspects, typically will be the one who excels. Many quarterbacks have strong arms. Is this the only thing one needs to be great? No. They need to be leaders. They need to have accuracy. They need to be tough. They need to be smart and know the plays and read defenses. The point is that these are the details, the intangibles that separate athletes who have similar physical skills.

23.

Starting Is Often The Hardest

"Don't let life discourage you; everyone who got
where he is had to begin where he was."
- Richard L. Evans

This is a concept I am sure most of you are already familiar with. You plan to workout tomorrow. You wake up and just don't feel like it during the day. However, something just triggers in you and you decide just to go to the gym and do a quick workout since it will be better then nothing. An hour later you are done with a very good workout.

Just starting something is often the hardest part. Most of the time if you go to the gym, good things will happen. If you decide to take a short jog, once you are doing it, you will feel better and have a good run. If you don't, it is still better then doing nothing. Tom Cruise was not the Tom Cruise we all know until he got a start in his first role. He didn't get his first role until he decided to become an actor. That decision, to pursue a career that has a great deal of failure, was the hardest part of the whole process. Next was continuing to do commercials, smaller roles, plays, whatever it took, to get himself in the position where he could audition for movie roles. He finally got his shot, after many rejections, and then made the most of the opportunity.

It is not easy to meet new people, especially in places such as nightclubs where everyone wants to meet the right person but is completely afraid of rejection. Having the courage to break the ice and meet new people is often the step you need to take to create a long lasting relationship that can bring a lifetime of joy. Saying hello, starting, is the often the hardest part.

24.
Body Language

"The journey of a thousand miles begins with one step."
- Lao-Tse

While I am not a scientist, I certainly know many of the major theories. One is that ninety percent of all communication is considered to be non-verbal. How others perceive us is crucial in many aspects of life. But even more so it has a lot to do with controlling our attitude and emotions. If you smile, you feel a bit better. All too often when faced with adversity during competition, many athletes will tell you exactly how they feel, just by their body language--slumped shoulders, head down, slower movements. This is not what will turn around your play. This is not what will inspire teammates. This is not what will give your coach confidence. While many athletes get so excited when they are doing well and so upset when not, the more even keeled one can be, the more they can withstand adversity. Tom Glavine is a perfect example. If you turn on a game where he is pitching and did not see the score, it would be impossible to tell if he is winning or losing, throwing a no-hitter or getting shelled. This does not mean he is not passionate or emotional, it just means that he is in control.

This may not work for all of us, but if you can at least attempt to keep your body language in a positive manner when things are going badly, you will have a better chance to turn things around.

25.

Let Others Have Spotlight/Be Humble

*"Most of the trouble in the world is caused by people
who want to be important."*
- T.S. Eliot

*"Be nice to people on your way up
because you meet them on your way down."*
- Jimmy Durante

It is well known that when you give, you also receive. It is also well known that no one likes a showoff. Sure, it takes confidence and courage to be a top player. But when you reach that level, chances are you did not do it alone. The more you are thankful for what you have achieved and give others the credit, the more love they will give back to you. When you tell people how good you are, it turns them off. You didn't invent the sport. You are not the first one to hit a home run or score a touchdown. Sure you can celebrate, after all it is what you worked for. But share your joy, don't talk about how good you are.

There is also an interesting paradox in regard to being a humble person. The more you brag and try to tell others how good you are, the more they get turned off and resent you for bragging. Yet the more you deflect the praise and stay humble in the spotlight, the more others will appreciate you.

26.
Be Coachable

"If you think education is expensive, try ignorance."
-Derek Bok.

A man who had been bypassed for a promotion went to the president and complained, saying that he had fifteen years of experience with the firm. The president answered him, "Not so. You have had one year of experience fifteen times."

The best players are always the best learners. Players who are coachable are always trying to learn more about being successful players and people. While you might not agree with what your coach or teacher says, give it a shot and if you don't like it, don't do it. But don't say you know before you try. If one coach tell you one thing and another tells you differently, it does not mean that one is right and the other wrong. Both probably have merit. Give each way a shot and do what you feel is the best.

In the business world, some companies use what is called 360 degree feedback. That is, managers are evaluated by their bosses, those they work with, those that work for them, and finally by themselves. Then the feedback from all those sources is put into a training program to help them improve

Besides your coaches, you can ask other players on your team what they think of you. It might be what they think are the parts of your game you need to improve. Could you be more of a hustler on the field? Whatever it might be. If you are reluctant to do just what your coach says, it might hit home more when you hear it from a teammate, friend, and peer.

This can also be taken further. Being coachable also means being responsible for your own education and improvement as a player. If your coach does not have the expertise or time to devote to your game, you may have to read articles or books, watch videos, or find your own coach or instructor to improve.

27.
If You Say You Can't, You Can't

"Whether you think that you can, or that you can't,
you are usually right."
- Henry Ford

"Things are only impossible until they are not."
- Jean Luc Picard, Star Trek:
The Next Generation

"Those who say it can't be done are usually
interrupted by others doing it."
- Joel A. Barker

If you say that you can, it doesn't mean you will, but certainly that you will try. If you say you can't, however, it really does mean that you can't. If you say you have a limitation then you do. If you know for sure you can't shoot three pointers, I can bet that you can't. If you are willing to work on it and try to get better, then you might be able to. Maybe you are not ready to try it during the game, but that you will come an hour before or after practice and shoot until you get better at it. But the moment you say you can't, even if you just say it to yourself, then you can't. No one ran the four minute mile until one person did. Now many runners can do it. When you say you can't there is no chance. When you say you can, there is. You can either complain that rose bushes have thorns, or be happy that thorn bushes have roses. If you say you can't get a woman like that, you can't. If you say you can't get a job like that, you won't. But if you think, I might be able get a man like that or a house like that, then the doors are still open to achieve your dreams.

28.
Build Good Habits

"The best way to break a habit is to drop it."
- Bartig

*"Good habits are as addictive as bad habits,
and a lot more rewarding."*
- Harvey Mackay

We are creatures of habit. This is normal. Habits bring order to an often-confusing world. However, habits can be either positive or negative. Smoking, drinking, taking drugs, and over eating are obviously all bad habits. Eating right, getting up early, and exercising are all good habits. The interesting fact is that both are just as addicting. The person who never took an aerobics class, if they last a month or so after they start, will be hooked for good. If they can't make a class for whatever reason, they will feel upset. Ideally you need to start working towards eliminating your bad habits and building better ones.

Good habits make us better performers. Sure, the piano player would much rather play an interesting piece by Bach, but she knows that doing scales every day is the root to her best performance. As it relates to sports, creating good habits is essential. Shooting 100 free throws, making 100 putts, taking 100 baseball swings, watching film, jogging, eating right, whatever it might be for you, the more positive habits that you can create, the better you will be.

The best way you can move from negative to positive behaviors is in small steps. Though stopping things cold turkey or starting good habits in an instant can work for some, the rest of us need to stop the bad things and build the good things in gradual increments.

29.
Play Each Play Like It Is Your Last

"Eat, drink, and be merry, for tomorrow we die."
- Dave Matthews

"Dream as if you'll live forever. Live as if you'll die tomorrow."
- James Dean

If I told you that you were going to die tomorrow, would you treat this day any differently? I am sure you would in so many ways. Well, here is a secret. You are going to die tomorrow. If not tomorrow, then the next day. If not the next day, then in a few next days. About the only thing we know for sure in this world is that we are going to die. Yet most of us live as if we are going to live forever. If you are in a fight with a friend, would you treat that fight the same way if you knew you were going to die tomorrow? I doubt it.

Take this frame of mind to the field. If you knew this was your last game, how would you play it? Would you be as aware as possible, soaking it all in, doing the best that you could? What if I was able to predict your last pitch, or throw, or stroke, or shot? Would you treat it differently? I imagine so. Give it your all, so that when it does become your last game, your last play, you will not say, "I could have, I should have, I would have." You will say, "I did."

If you had a chance to listen to all those that can no longer play the sport due to injury, my guess is that what they would tell you is to play like each play is the last, because it could be. Each time you say goodbye to your parents, make it like it might be the last time, because it could be. Often we get into the perspective that our jobs, athletic careers, and our lives will go on forever. Yet by realizing and living in a way that recognizes that nothing lasts forever, will make you appreciate all you have today.

30.
Get A Mentor

"Every man's work is a portrait of himself."
- Jose Ortega y Gasset

Everyone needs a coach. You have several choices. It can simply be the coach you now have. It can be a friend. It can be another player on the team. It can be a teacher or parent. Maybe it is someone you don't know yet, but that you really respect. You can ask that person how they achieved what they did, so that you can try and follow the same path. You can even become your own coach. Maybe you lack the technical knowledge to improve your skills, but you can certainly become your own coach in terms of effort and motivation. Being your own coach means being aware of your thoughts. It means controlling the thoughts in our mind. We constantly talk to ourselves all the time. If it is true that we become what we think, and I believe it is, then it makes sense to control what we are thinking. If you are too tired to get out of bed for your early morning workout, you can step back and become your own coach and psychologist. Why is it so hard? What can you do to change? Maybe you go to bed too late, or that you are so used to going back to sleep. You could create a solution to put your alarm clock on the other side of the room. This way, when it goes off, you have to get out of bed. Then for a week you will not go back to bed or do a workout, but simply get used to being awake at an early hour. Once you are able to do this, then you will do a light workout in the morning. Once you are able to do that, then you will do a full-fledged workout.

31
When

*"The haves and the have-nots can often be traced back
to the dids and the did-nots."*
- D.O. Flynn

The great singer-songwriter Dave Matthews knows about this. One of his songs goes, "I can't believe that we would lie in our graves, dreaming of things that we might have been." He should know. He was inches from never being a musician at all. It took so much time, practice, and courage to explore his creative side. The voice of his late Dad was always saying inside his head, "Get a job. Get a job." Thank God he didn't. I would have nothing to listen to.

A day doesn't go by when I don't here someone say how if they knew then what they know now, how much different life would be. For so many of us, we don't take that risk or dream to be great since we don't want to try our best and fail. Our mindset is that if we haven't given it our all, then when we don't get what we wanted, we really haven't lost all that much. What a shame to think that way. If you are not going to start eating properly right now, when are you?

If you are not going to commit to a workout program now, when are you? If you are not going to learn the way the coach wants it done now, when are you?

We put off so many things in our lives for reasons that make little sense. I will start eating right after the holidays. I will start working out after the season. I don't have time to watch film now, but I will get to it. Why wait? Make the changes you want today and stick to them.

32.
Be Aware Of Excuses

"Ninety-nine percent of the failures come from people who have the habit of making excuses."
- George Washington Carver

Just about every time we make excuses, we deter our growth as people and players. When we blame teammates, equipment, field conditions, coaches, and umpires for our performance, we miss the opportunity to learn from our mistakes. In essence, we deny our mistakes since we do not want to accept responsibility for them. If you do not accept responsibility, how are you going to better yourself and improve? If you are a quarterback and you throw an interception, but instead of admitting you misread the defense and threw a bad pass, you blame your receiver for running the wrong route, the offensive line for not giving you enough time, the coach for calling the play, or the wind effect on the ball, you miss the chance to learn from your mistake and do better the next time.

In addition, don't accept the excuses that others offer you regarding your performance. Whether it be a friend, parent, teammate, or coach, allowing another to take away your responsibility does the same thing as if you offered up the excuse yourself. If your dad tells you that the interception wasn't your fault because the team is using the wrong type of football, and you accept that, you again miss the real reason you made a poor throw and thus the chance to learn from it. You are not expected to be a perfect performer, but if your goal is to improve, then you need to acknowledge that you failed and then take steps to ensure that mistake does not happen again. Sports are not easy. You will make mistakes. Just accept them and work harder. For many, excuses are simply a way of avoiding hard work.

33.

Have Honor

"No amount of ability is of the slightest avail without honor."
- Andrew Carnegie

Those that get the most out of athletics are those that are honorable. Learning these characteristics will serve you well in any area of life. Being honorable means that you are always giving your all. You hustle all the time, encourage your teammates, you don't talk badly about another team or coach or player. You show respect to officials. You pick up your teammates when they are down. You do not lose control and throw equipment or fight a teammate. You don't distract an opponent with cheap antics. You don't run trick plays. Show everyone your values by the way you practice and play.

Having honor means doing what is right when no one is looking. It means never cheating on a test or a paper. It means never stealing or littering or being mean for no reason. Having honor means you don't steal at work, you don't get tempted by insider trading or cooking the accounting books. You realize that all your actions have effects on others and more importantly, on your soul.

34.
Be Relentless

"O Lord, Thou givest us everything, at the price of an effort."
- Leonardo Da Vinci

"The heights by great men reached and kept were not attained by sudden flight, but they, while their companions slept, were toiling upward in the night."
- Henry Wadsworth Longfellow

As long as you are in a game, a contest, an event, never give up. If you are losing by a wide margin, you should play the game the same way. If you are winning by a lot, you should also play the game the same. Be the player on the team, that even though you might lose by a large margin, the players and coaches on the other team know your name and number. Do not allow your teammates to give up. Never let anyone give up in a game. Demand that the officials judge the game in the same way regardless of the score. A game is a game, it should be played all out regardless of the score or situation. If you are a runner in a marathon, you don't slow down if you are in front, just the way you don't slow down because you are last. You run the best you can until the end. The other team cannot make you quit. No one can. This does not mean that you play the game without mental regard to the score. There are certain strategies that have to be executed in order to keep a lead or catch up, however, this does not affect the effort that you give. Give all you can for as long as you can and then enjoy the effort you gave as you build to the next event. You don't lose, you simply run out of time. The other team may be better then your team, but your opponent does not have to be better then you. If the rest of your team misses all their tackles, then you make all the tackles. If the rest of your team cannot hit, you get the only hits. If the others on your team rest because the game is in hand, you remind them with your play how quickly things can turn and thus you should never let up. When your team rests because they are winning and have lost the desire to work as hard, you remind them how easy you can be dethroned without persistent work. You will, regardless of score, record, or situation, be the one who plays hard throughout.

35.

Be Present
(One Shot/Serve/Pitch/Play At A Time)

*"One of the most tragic things I know about human nature is
that all of us tend to put off living. We are all dreaming of some
magical rose garden over the horizon instead of enjoying the roses
that are blooming outside our windows today."*
- Dale Carnegie

When in a game, if you are reliving past plays in your head or focusing on something that will not take place until way later in the game (an at bat, for example) then you will not be prepared for now. And, now is all we have. Your sole job when you play is to be prepared for the present moment. What do you do if they blitz on this play? What if they pass the ball to me? What if the ball is hit to me? What if the goalie comes out? That is the proper present moment thinking. Even if you are not in the game at the moment, there is a good chance that you will get in. Will you be prepared? Are you actively watching and focused on the game and learning how to do the best job when you are out there, or are you simply wasting time hoping to be called upon? Teams and players have tendencies and you can learn a great deal by watching them.

What happened earlier in the game is of small use at the present. Whether it was good or bad, your goal should be to do as well as you can right now. If you haven't gotten one hit all day, it is tough to get one if you keep focusing on the previous at bats. If you have gotten four hits, that is not going to help you if that is all you are focused on. This at-bat is the only one of consequence. When the game is over, of course you can review your entire game, but not while the game is being played. Avoid looking in the stands, do not talk to friends, to parents, stay focused.

36.
Focus On Task, Not On The Result

"Happiness is essentially a state of going somewhere,
wholeheartedly, one-directionally, without regret or reservation."
- William H. Sheldon

Again, this is under the realm of how you cannot control much outside your own effort. If you are simply concerned and focused on a result, it is often hard to achieve. Thoughts such as; "I have to make this shot. I have to get a hit. This has to go in the hole. I have to make this kick", can get you into trouble since they put pressure on you to get a result as opposed to doing the thing necessary to get the result. In other words, instead of focusing on the fact that you have to make the field goal, it is better off to remind yourself to be relaxed, keep your head down and drive through the ball. If you do those things properly, then chances are that the kick will be a good one.

You might be playing golf in a match against someone who is shooting a tremendously low score. Focusing on getting low scores just to keep up with them is wrong. You need to play the match with the goal of hitting each shot the best you possibly can, each time, and if you do this, you will give your best effort. If your best effort is good enough to beat your opponent, so be it. If not, you still gave your 100% effort and played as hard and focused as you could. This can be taken further to thinking about each individual swing. You may have hit the ball perfectly, right at the hole, but it hits the flag stick and bounces into a sand trap. You could hit a bird, the cart path, a stick, get a bad lie, or whatever. Throw a good pitch and don't worry about the strikeout. The point is to focus more on the moment and the effort that you are giving, then on the outcome.

37.
Simplify

"The more you get, the more you get to take care of."
- Alice K. Dormann

"Success is getting what you want;
happiness is wanting what you get."
- Dale Carnegie

The key to success in athletics is the elimination of bad habits. This is especially true in the actions that are more mechanical. Baseball/softball hitting and throwing, basketball shooting, tennis and golf, much of swimming, and track and field are perfect examples. Much of performing these skills to your potential is to eliminate the extra that is complicating the action. Simplifying our skills allows our true abilities to emerge.

The same holds true for other areas of our life. The more we can simplify our lives we get closer to finding what really matters. Sure it might be nice to have five cars. But soon you will realize that all the time and effort and expense that it takes to own, insure, and keep them will take away the energy that could be used in other areas of your life. Often we are possessed by our possessions instead of the other way around. The more stuff we have, the more effort it takes to keep that stuff. As George Carlin jokes "As soon as you have more room, you get more stuff." I am certainly not going to go as far as saying that you can't be a good player if you room is messy, but it is just another issue you really don't need to worry about.

My grandmother hardly ever gave me advice about life, she was just a wonderful woman and I learned a lot by watching her. The answer to whatever ailed me was moderation. Whether it was eating or exercise or alcohol or dating, whatever, I learned that having balance in life and showing moderation was the way to lead a long and happy life. She surely did.

38.
Doing What You Always Do
Get What You Always Get

"There are two kinds of men who never amount to much - those who cannot do what they are told and those who can do nothing else."
- Cyrus H.L. Curtis

*"Show me a man who cannot bother to do the little things
and I'll show you a man who cannot be trusted to big things."*
- Lawrence D. Bell

This can be a positive or a negative. If you are experiencing success, chances are that most of what you are doing to prepare for your performance is right. It is working. Stick with the way you are approaching your practices, training, and competition. While you should not rest and still need to work hard, winning/playing well is direct feedback for the preparation you have been doing. If you hope to shoot a 70 on a certain golf course and set your practice regimen to meet that goal, and then you go out and shoot a 68, more then likely, what you have been doing to practice and prepare has been working.

However, if the opposite is true and you are continuing to perform below your expectations, you may see, upon further inspection, that your preparation needs change. For example, if you realize that you are not a strong as you need to be and that is affecting your performance, you have two choices. If you do what you have always done, in this case, not push yourself hard enough in the weight room, then you will continue to be deficient in strength. If you change the routine you do, workout with a partner who can push you harder, or simply decide that what you have been doing will no longer cut it and it is time to workout harder, you will find that a new devotion will lead to the strength gains you need. These gains will more then likely increase your performance on the court, in the pool, or wherever you perform. If X = Y and you like Y, keep doing X. If you are not happy with Y, you would be silly to continue to do X and expect to get other then Y. Turn the equation to X +H + N = Y.

39.
Change Happens In An Instant

"Experience is not what happens to you;
it is what you do with what happens to you."
-Aldous Huxley

Whether it's for better or worse, don't underestimate how quickly life can change. If you are single, for example, and have been frustrated for the last six months because you have been hoping to meet the right person, yet it does not seem to be happening. Your life can change in an evening when you go to a party and get introduced to the person who becomes your wife. The phone can ring one day with a new job offer that requires a move across the country.

However, the type of change I am referring to in athletics is mostly in regard to your emotional control during competition. More then ever in these days of "road rage," I see more and more of parents, coaches, and players losing control on the field. Getting into fights, throwing equipment with the intent to hurt, or any another offense that can hurt, or even kill others can forever change your life. Sports are supposed to be fun. While many games can get heated, it is never right to fight. Fists can kill. Baseballs and bats can kill. Kicks can injure. Coaches have hit players, players have fought with fans, players have seriously hurt other players, and players have punched officials. Careers can end in an instant. Athletics can turn from a fun competition to a court case very quickly. Prepare yourself for the eventual adversity that can make you lose your temper and plan to act calmly in the face of what, in the moment, can feel like life or death.

The way you drive, a plane flight, a night out at a bar, all of these things can change your life in an instant. Drive drunk and hurt someone in an accident and your life will never be the same. What can seem as a harmless few drinks and then a short drive home, can put you behind bars, cost you your job, money, family, and freedom. Actions have consequences. Think it through.

40.
Do What You Know

"If I had my life to live again,
I'd make the same mistakes, only sooner."
- Tallulah Bankhead

"The most difficult thing in the world is to know how to do a thing
and to watch someone else doing it wrong, without commenting."
- T.H. White

"Wisdom consists in knowing what to do with what you know."
- Diogenes Laertius

When an athlete seeks to improve, the job of a coach is to do the following; First, identify the part of their game causing them a problem. Next is to establish the proper skill that needs to replace the old way. Finally, is to give the athlete the steps, drills, and advice that will make this change a lasting one. Thus, the key for any athlete is knowing what to do. However, even once you established exactly what needs to be worked on, not all players will do what they know needs to be done. It is the same for the person who knows they need to stop overeating. They know they need to stop, they have been given ways to reach this goal, but they still cannot do it. We know that to eat better we should shop healthier and stock our refrigerator with healthy food choices. We know this. It is very simple. Yet, when we go to the supermarket, especially when hungry, we wind up getting lots of snack and junk food that we can always pick from around the house. In essence, although we know what to do, we have a hard time doing it.

The best athletes are the ones that can make these type of changes. The ones that are able to put the knowledge they have been given to full use. They are able to do what they know. If a boxer constantly drops his right hand when he makes a jab with his left, a good opponent will eventually throw a hard left hand just as the jab is thrown. The first step is to know that the right hand must stay up when punching to protect against a counterpunch. The next step is to build drills around this exact task. The first one could be 500 jabs a day against a heavy bag, all while concentrating on keeping the right hand up. Next, the boxer could practice with a trainer who uses a hand pad to take the fighter's jab while at the same time using a punching pad to hit his boxer in the face on each jab. Either he will connect if not done right, or hopefully soon the fighter learns that if he wants to avoid getting hit in the face, he needs to keep his hand up. With enough practice and dedication, eventually he will learn this skill, which could be the difference in his whole boxing career. Almost every sport has similar issues and the premier athletes will find flaws and then spend all their time and energy fixing them. Even if the remedy is boring or monotonous to perform, they know it will build muscle memory which is the key to change.

41.
Sports And Life Are A Gift

"Do you know what my favorite part of the game is?
The opportunity to play."
-Mike Singletary

"I love the winning, I can take the losing,
but most of all I love to play."
- Boris Becker

It is fair to say that many of us take much in our lives for granted. If you take time to contemplate our universe and the fact that there is even life on Earth, it might make you gain a new perspective and not get so caught up in the little things that ruin our experience of it. We will always have struggles in life, but we allow many things to aggravate us that don't need to. The day is going along fine, but then all of sudden you get a bill in the mail that overcharges you. Instead of staying calm, knowing that the issue will be solved, you let it drive you nuts. If the issue does eventually get solved, then all the time you took to let it upset you is lost and can never be regained. Even if you don't get the issue fixed, is it really worth it, to get so upset that you ruin your time on the planet? I don't mean to say that nothing should ever bother you, in fact, frustration has led to many great developments in our history. However, you can vow to fix things, without having them control your life. If you knew you were going to die tomorrow, would that bill bother you today?

I believe that sports are a gift that should not be taken for granted. The opportunity to practice and play a game is a privilege, one that many never get to experience. It should not be taken lightly, rather experienced to the fullest. There are those that cannot play due to injury or other health problems, who would love a chance to play. If even just for those people we owe it to never take for granted our ability to run, jump, throw, catch, and play. There may soon be a day when you will no longer be in school or on a team, or in a league where you can hit, shoot, catch, or pass and you will regret it if you let your chances pass you by.

42.

Passion

"If one advances confidently in the direction of his dreams,
and endeavors to live the life which he has imagined,
he will meet with a success unexpected in common hours."
- Henry David Thoreau

"Do what you love to do and give it your very best.
Whether it's business or baseball, or the theater, or any field.
If you don't love what you're doing and you can't give it
your best, get out of it. Life is too short. You'll be an old man
before you know it."
- Al Lopez

Most people will agree that passion is where it all starts. Whether it
be running a business, climbing a mountain, writing a book, passion
is really what keeps us moving toward our goals. Passion is created
through goals and dreams. Why work hard? Why study film? Why
get good grades? Why jog in the morning and lift weights at night?
Why stay away from drugs? Why be coachable? If your goal is to
run a full length marathon and you have a passion to finish the race

to prove to yourself that you can achieve high goals, then this is the motivation to get you to run on a regular basis. You cannot run a marathon if you don't run at least five days a week. When it is raining, and most people would just skip the run, if you are passionate about reaching your goal, you will put on your rain coat and go. Whether your goal is to make the team, get more playing time, become a starter, perform better, reach certain statistics, win games, win championships, having this end goal is mind will give you the passion to overcome adversity since it is just a bump on the road to your dreams.

43.
If You Don't Work To Failure, You Are Failing To Work

"A widely prevalent notion today seems to demand instant achievement of goals, without any of the wearying, frustrating preparation that is indispensable to any task. As the exemplar way of life, the professional - that man or woman who injects every new task or duty, no matter how small, with discipline of mind and spirit - is a vanishing American, particularly among those

who too often believe that dreams come true because they
ought to and not because they are caused to materialize"
- Jack Valenti

"The pessimist sees the difficulty in every opportunity;
the optimist, the opportunity in every difficulty."
- L.P. Jacks

There are several stages of being an athlete. For some, just getting in the game or making the team is fine. Sports are a small part of their life and while they like playing, it is not a passion. Their passion might be studies, business, music, art, whatever. They put in a fair effort, but seldom a great one. They don't push as hard as they can in practice because they don't have a burning desire to get better. They play because they enjoy it, but not as a challenge of how good they can be.

Some of you, however, want to be the best you can be. Being good is not good enough. You expect more from yourself. You might be a high school football player with a goal to play at a Division I college. The football season is ten games. The year is 365 days. This means you have 355 days to prepare to show the world what you can do. While it is not realistic to lift weights, condition, and practice each and every day, it is important that when you do, you push yourself to failure. If the day's workout is to run sprints, then run them until you can't run anymore. The player who just wants to be average will not run at all, or run five 50 yard dashes. Your workout should be running ten 10's, ten 20's, ten 30's, ten 40's, ten 50's, ten 60's, ten 70's. ten 80's, ten 90's, and ten 100's. If you can't do that much, do as much until you can't run any more. If that amount is too little, keep running. If you do this, the game will be easy for you. If the game goes into overtime and those around you are beat, you will not be.

44.
Small In The Way Of Big

"People are always blaming their circumstance for what they are. I don't believe in circumstances. The people who get on in this world are the people who look for the circumstances they want, and if they can't find them, make them."
- George Bernard Shaw

As a college baseball coach, I believe that it is crucial that my players play baseball in the summer time. Anyone who wants to compete at the college level must play as much as possible to improve. This is even more important if they have a goal of playing baseball for a living after college. Yet often during the end of the year meetings, I would ask players what they plan to do and many would say that they could not play in the summer because they had to work. When I asked why they had to work, the answers ranged from earning spending money for school, paying for a car, gas money, car insurance, etc. So they spend all their time in the summer working at a meaningless minimum wage job to earn $2,500.

Now I am certainly not saying that working is not important, it is. I am also not claiming that many kids don't need to make money to help their family. What I am saying is that if instead of being college athletes, they were already multi-million dollar athletes, what would they do during their off-season? To a player, they all would say that they would workout and work on their hitting, pitching, throwing, and fielding.

My point was, why don't you treat yourself as this type of player now? If they don't, they will have less of a chance reaching their goals. There will be a lifetime to work should baseball not be their career. There is only one time to play college baseball. I suggested that they either find a better way to make money (such as instructing young kids on baseball or coaching a team) or that they take a loan from family or friend that will help with their expenses and they will pay this person back after college.

Sometimes we all lose our site of our big goal by getting caught up in the small things on the way. When there is passion, a will, there is a way.

45.

Visualize

*"It's how you deal with failure
that determines how you achieve success."*
-Dave Feherty

Different from meditation or other forms of clearing your mind and relaxing, visualization is an active technique that can prepare you to achieve better levels of play and help you reach your goals. In one form, visualization is practice. If there are plays or tasks you need to remember come game time, going through them first in your mind is one source of practice. It can also be used as performance preparation. You can go through all the skills you will need in a game. For example, if you play quarterback, you can visualize taking the snap from center, doing handoffs properly, avoiding the rush, scrambling for first downs, throwing the ball accurately, and making good decisions. Again, it is a way of preparing yourself for all the skills you will need during the course of a game. Taken a step further, you can also prepare yourself on how to emotionally handle situations. You can come into the game with the bases loaded before it ever actually happens. You can mentally see yourself warming up, jogging in, taking your warm up pitches and being calm. Then visualize yourself getting the hitters out.

There is only so much time we can physically practice or get into a game, thus visualization is another form of practice and preparation. The process of visualization can take many forms. You can put yourself into your own shoes and imagine that you are performing the tasks that you will eventually need during competition. You can also try more of a projection technique, whereby you actually use your mind's eye to imagine you are doing the tasks on a TV or film screen. Finally, you can try more of a "bird's eye" view, where you are seeing yourself perform from a higher up perspective. No one way is wrong or right, just different.

46.
Becoming Great Can Separate You

*"You stop worrying about what other people think about you
when you realize how little they do."*
- Mark Twain

*"Do not follow where the path may lead.
Go instead where there is no path and leave a trail."*
- Muriel Strode

*"To be nobody but myself, in a world that is doing its best, night and
day, to make you everybody else, means to fight the hardest battle
which any human being can fight, and never stop fighting."*
- EE Cummings

"Those who strive for great goals must risk rejection from their peers"
- John Noe

The average person does not have it in their will to be great. They simply do not want to do the work necessary to achieve that level of their potential. If you are going to be one that tries to reach this level, you may lose some friends along the way. You certainly don't have to, but it may happen. While your average athlete wants to play Nintendo, sleep, stay out late, drink, etc., you will be constantly working on your game. It does not mean that you can't spend time with your friends, but simply that you might not be doing all the things the average person does. Since coaches love to work with motivated players, you will find that the coaches give you special attention since they see that you require their best effort. Since you care so much, they will as well. This also can cause problems with teammates who see you as the coach's favorite. You will often be used as the example of how to do things properly, whether that be the effort that you give, the improvements that you have made, or the skill you possess, you will be a guiding example of how to do things right. Some will resent you for this. The friends you have who don't compete in athletics may never understand your dedication and focus. Soon you may find that they too resent you for being so driven. They will often try to bring you to their level, not in your best interest, but to make them feel better about themselves.

You may also find that some of your original mentors, teachers, parents, coaches, and peers, who once were a good source of motivation no longer understand your drive, nor do they have the knowledge to take you to the next level. Again, becoming great, having the relentless drive to be the best, can take you to a level where few understand what it is like to live that way. But it is the only way for you and risking losing some people along the way, while you hope it won't happen, may be a result of your drive. Don't alienate others, don't think less of them, or even better of yourself, just do what you need to do to achieve what you want and live the life you see for yourself. Your dedication and greatness will be there own reward.

47.
Make It Fun

"The only thing that keeps a man going is energy.
And what is energy but liking life?
- Louis Auchincloss

"He who laughs, lasts."
- Mary Pettibone Poole

"We do not stop playing because we are old.
We grow old because we stop playing."
- George Bernard Shaw

Never forget that the reason most of us love sports is we find the game and the competition fun. Anytime you can turn a practice or skill into a competition, you will find that it brings out the best in you and others. Even some tasks which might not be fun by nature can be made more interesting when done as a game. For example, you may not be able to jog because of your bad knee, but you can do the stairmaster. The boring way is to stare at the clocks until your workout is done and it is time to get off the machine. There are, however, ways in which you could make it more enjoyable. You could workout with a friend and talk. You could watch TV or a movie. You could read your favorite magazine or book (I like to get big print books from the library which are easier to read). You can listen to music or a book on tape. If you are lucky enough to have a view in your gym, just looking out the window is a peaceful way to pass the time. Whatever might work to help you get through something that you need is important.

While most of us play sports because they are fun, they are not always fun if not played well. So often I see people that I play golf with get very frustrated on the course. It is understandable to be frustrated by golf, or any sport for that matter, especially if you do not take the time to practice or get coaching. It seems silly to not take any golf lessons, never hit practice balls, and then get frustrated at shooting a 130. As you get instruction and actually work on your game it then makes more sense to have more interest in the outcome. No one likes to take lessons, spend hours on the driving range, and still shoot 130. So either play for total fun, or if you don't like your results, do something to improve them.

48.
New Age Is Current Age

"Failure is not fatal; failing to change will be."
- John Wooden

Many of the ideas that were once thought of as new age or weird simply are no longer viewed this way.

- Yoga, the art of increasing strength, flexibility, while calming the mind is a great way to prepare for any sport. Being flexible is the key to injury prevention, it builds strength in muscles, joints, and ligaments, and teaches patience and relaxation.
- Meditation, the art of quieting the mind, is now also thought of as a great way to relax and recover, but also to prepare for a prac-

tice or game. Since our minds are constantly working, thinking, meditation is the art of non-thinking.

- Pilates is a popular way to build strength through the core of your body and elongate your muscles.
- Karate and Tai Chi can also teach balance of the body and peacefulness of the mind.
- Becoming much more popular in recent years is the art of balance and core training. You often see athletes train with blow up balls and a variety of devices to increase balance.

Every sport requires balance, strength, flexibility, and total body awareness and some of the ideas above are ideal ways to achieve these skills.

49.
Give Back

"Happiness is the only good. The time to be happy is now.
The place to be happy is here. The way to be happy
is to make others so."
- Robert G. Ingersoll

"What lies behind us and what lies before us are tiny matters compared to what lies within us."
- Ralph Waldo Emerson

"Just think how happy you'd be if you lost have right now - and then got it back again."
- Bertrand Russell

It is important that at some point you give back to others some of what you have received through sports. It takes a lot more then you may have considered to run a team at any level. First off, coaches are dedicated to helping you grow as an athlete or person. While many coaches are paid well, often they could be making a better living in another way. Many coaches are volunteers who work full time in other jobs and give their time and energy to help. For you to have played all these years many people have been very giving. Your parents have given much just to raise you, let alone give their time, money, and energy to your athletic interests. Your teammates, many who worked hard with less talent then you. Umpires and officials deserve a lot of credit. While you might find that you only complain about the job they do, often they are very good. But more importantly how would a game go without them? If no one wanted to umpire little league baseball, there would be no little league baseball. Administrators also do a great deal of work, most of it behind the scenes. They help get fields ready, make schedules, get equipment, hire coaches, make sure athletes are healthy and cared for, and much, much more. Then there are trainers, fans, bus drivers, reporters, ticket takers, parking attendants, vendors, public address announcers, and the list goes on and on. Much goes into organized sports. When you get the chance to help others get the same experience you did, take advantage of it. It might be to become a referee, teach a youth group, donate money to a fundraising cause, or speak to a group. Whatever you can do to keep the cycle going is not just kind, it should be expected of you.

50.
Show Respect

"Hate is like acid. It can damage the vessels in which it is stored as well as destroy the object on which it is poured."
- Ann Landers

"Now, I say to you today my friends, even though we face the difficulties of today and tomorrow, I still have a dream. It is a dream deeply rooted in the American dream. I have a

dream that one day this nation will rise up and live out
the true meaning of its creed: we hold these truths to be
self-evident, that all men are created equal."
- Martin Luther King, Jr.

It is crucial that you show respect to those around you throughout your life and athletic career. Coaches, teammates, administrators, fans, equipment manager, janitors, and so on deserve respect. If you leave the locker room a mess, remember someone has to clean it up. If the janitor has to do it, how would you feel if that janitor was your father or grandfather. Never treat others as less then you. One of your teammates could become president or own a great company. Don't burn your britches and remember, those you see on the way up will be there on the way down.

If you want respect, you need to give respect, not just demand it. You cannot treat a friend, a teammate, a coach, a teacher, a boss, a parent, a wife, an umpire without respect and simply just demand that they respect you. Life does not work that way. You earn respect the way you treat others, the way you practice, the way you work, play, and live.

51.
Other Source of Inspiration

"So many of our dreams at first seem impossible. And then they seem improbable. And then, when we summon the will, they soon become inevitable."
- Christopher Reeve

"You are the only person on earth who can use your ability."
- Zig Ziglar

There are many ways to find motivation and inspiration. You can read books about your sport, either technical ways to improve or stories by those who have achieved or overcome. You can read general books about success or effort. There are plenty of magazines which have motivational stories such as Sports Illustrated, Fortune, or Time. For many, a quality movie is very inspirational. Who could watch Rocky and not want to box? What baseball player doesn't love The Natural or Field of Dreams? Hoosiers, Rudy, Good Will Hunting, the list goes on. The internet is a source for a great deal of information. Educational television can motivate you. Those who watch cooking shows often want to cook better. You watch the home networks, it makes you want to repair your kitchen. If you watch ESPN's biographies on the great athletes, this might inspire you to become one. Tiger Woods wanted to be like Jack Nicklaus, now how many want to be like Tiger Woods?

How many bands did Elvis Presley influence? How many baseball players love Roger Clemens and wanted to grow up and be just like him?

For many people their parents are motivational. Seeing how hard they work at unsung jobs, even second jobs, making ends meet, and raising kids, is very inspirational. For others their kids are a source of motivation. If your children are active, I am sure you would like to keep up with them. You certainly want to be around for them as long as you can.

While I typically don't prefer to use negative means as a source of motivation, it certainly can work. If you are obese, read statistics about life span. If you are a smoker, research the effects of cancer and emphysema. Having a problem with drugs, just watch Cops or visit your local jail. Our choices add up to become who we are.

52.
Fuel

"Nothing motivates a man more than to see his boss putting in an honest day's work."
-Louis? Wain

"I am only one. But still I am one. I cannot do everything, but still I can do something. And because I cannot do everything, I will not refuse to do the something that I can do."
- Edward E Hale

Would you put cheap gas in a BMW? Give pizza to a horse? I doubt it. Fact is, the human body is the greatest of all machines. It will not work well without the right fuel. Your computer will not go on without a battery or electricity, nor will your body run without the proper nutrition. Small, frequent meals, with a balance between protein, carbohydrates, and fat are optimal. Stay away from too much sugar. Drink water instead of soda, juices, or coffee. Save your money on sports drinks and drink water instead. Don't get too caught up in any one fad about nutrition. Moderation has been and will always be the key. Eating just protein, no fat, whatever the diet or fad might be, is not going to be your answer in the long run.

Many athletes have problems with alcohol. Don't binge drink. Learn to stay away from drinking or at least drink in moderation. Learn to have a few drinks and have fun, without having to have twelve beers and be hung over. Stay away from smoking, tobacco, and drugs. If you have a problem with any of these, find a counselor. You can be a partier, a great athlete, but not both. It's your choice.

If you are tempted to take a performance-enhancing drug such as steroids, do your research. If you do, you will find that you are seeking short-term gains for a lifetime of trouble. Will steroids increase your strength and often your performance? Yes they will. Is it the edge that can get to you the next level? Yes. Can they shorten your life span, give you emotional and physical problems? That has proven to be the case. Besides steroids there are also a host of other enhancement type products on the market, most sold at nutritional stores right over the counter. The fact is that these companies get them on the market way faster then the FDA can give them a long term study. You are better off gaining your physique from old fashioned hard work and food that God put on the planet, not drugs that have to be engineered in a lab. Again the choice is yours.

53.
Rest and Recovery

*"Sometimes the most urgent and vital thing you
can possibly do is take a complete rest.*
- Ashleigh Brilliant

*"Sometimes when I consider what tremendous consequences come
from little things, I am tempted to think there are no little things."*
- Bruce Barton

If you are one that pushes yourself to the limit in both practice and games, you will need proper rest and recovery. On the most basic level this means getting adequate sleep. Training or competing on a lack of sleep will eventually hurt your performance. I am not referring to the night before the big game when you can't sleep. Your adrenaline will take over when you need it. But the night after the big event, you had better get your rest to get you back on track. On a regular basis you need to have a solid sleeping pattern to perform well.

Other methods can help you relax both your body and mind as well. Taking a hot bath, getting a message, writing in a journal, relaxing by candlelight, even taking a long shower while alternating between hot and cold water will help get you ready and avoid burnout. They often can be something to look forward to and be used as a reward for a hard earned effort. If you are constantly going, going, going, you may soon find that you lose interest in your sport. So often we hear of young tennis or ice skating stars that practice hours and hours, but have little time for fun and rest. All work and no play makes Johnny a dull boy. Watch a movie, meditate, go on a slow hike, play with your dog, listen to music, it is your choice. Just know that the body and mind need to recharge and this should not be taken for granted. Often in the times of piece and quiet you will even find answers to things which had been of concern to you.

One of the simplest and most effective techniques to calm the mind and body is to simply breathe fully and deeply, in through the nose, out through the mouth, while concentrating on nothing but your breathing. So often our minds are just racing and thinking all the time, even when we sleep we dream, thus calming them with concentration on the breath can calm you in a very effective way.

54.
Nature Training

*"Courage is not the absence of fear, but rather the judgment
that something else is more important than fear."*
- Ambrose Redmoon

"Act the way you'd like to be and soon you'll be the way you act."
- George W. Crane

*"Nature has been for me, for as long as I remember,
a source of solace, inspiration, adventure,
and delight; a home, a teacher, a companion."*
- Lorraine Anderson

I have often found one of the best ways to train the body while relaxing the mind is to train in nature. Whatever is available near you will
work. Whether in the woods, on a mountain, by the ocean or lake,
anywhere that can put you in touch with nature will be inspirational
and peaceful. Gyms, with their weights and treadmills, are great and
have their purpose, but getting into nature is completely natural and
very beneficial. You can even try to do natural body/work exercise.

Push ups, sit ups, up hill sprints, put a log on your back and do squats, lift bags of sand, throw big rocks, do pull ups on a tree branch. You'll be surprised to find out how much of a workout this can be. Those who have worked on a farm, shoveled snow, or raked a yard of leaves know what I mean. Point is, don't just think the only workout you can get is in the gym. If you live in a city, find the nearest park or patch of grass, maybe there is even a waterfront to inspire you. It truly is therapeutic to be out of doors and in Mother Nature.

55.
Go Watch The Best

"To different minds, the same world is a hell, and a heaven."
- Ralph Waldo Emerson

*"There are some people who live in a dream world,
and there are some who face reality; and then there are
those who turn one into the other."*
- Douglas Everett

If you find that you need an extra source of motivation to get you going, I advise that you go and watch the best. If you are a team sport athlete, go find the best team in your area and watch to see what makes them so good. Watch the person at your position and see why he or she is so talented. Often times we simply compare ourselves to those players on our team. If you are much better then the rest of the team, you might feel that there is little work to be done. You might feel differently if you watch the best team in your area practice or play a game. It would also work if you went to watch the team at the next level. Maybe it is a higher conference team, or a college team, a minor league team, even a professional one. If you are in the pro's, watch the all-star game. If you are in the all-star game, keep up the good work. (Can you get back there next year?)

I have often found inspiration simply watching people do what they are great at. Though I am not good at soccer, I find it fascinating to watch a skilled player warm up by juggling the ball with her feet. I was amazed by Tiger Woods bouncing a golf ball off his club and then hitting it for the Nike commercial. One time in New York City I watched for an hour as two kids played spackle pails with drum sticks. I am blown away when I see someone break dance. Gymnastics fascinate me. The balance beam, the rings, the floor exercises, what an amazing show. Skaters, motorcycle riders, ski jumpers, jugglers, high wire walkers, the list goes on and on, all these people can inspire you to greatness. They show what humans can do if extreme focus is given to a particular skill.

56.
Be Aware of the Self-fulfilling Prophecy

*"Accept everything about yourself - I mean everything.
You are you and that is the beginning and the end -
no apologies, no regrets.*
- Clark Moustakas

*"If we have no winter, the spring would not be so pleasant:
if we did not sometimes taste of adversity, prosperity
would not be so welcome.*
- Anne Bradstreet

This concept is pretty simple. What we expect is often what we get. If you expect to run the mile in seven minutes, you are most likely going to run the mile in seven minutes. If you expect yourself to only reach a certain level of skill and performance, more then likely that is exactly what will happen. Since this is so, it makes a great deal of sense to give careful evaluation to your thoughts. While it might be unrealistic to expect to run the mile in four minutes, if you lower your expectations down to six minutes, you will be surprised at how your body will find ways to train and perform to help you get closer to your goal. If you say you can't hit a particular pitcher, then most likely you are right. If you say, I might be able to hit this pitcher, then work hard to do so, eventually you will be able to do it. The will finds the way.

Taken even further what a coach thinks regarding a player can often effect how that player turns out for the coach. This, known as the Pygmalion effect, has been studied in the classroom. A teacher was given two groups of children, one that read very well, one that did not. However, she was told that the group that did not read well were excellent readers, and the group that did read well, did not. Over the course of a given academic year, the group that did not read well made tremendous improvement over the group that did read well in the beginning. The point is, that if you are the third string quarterback, chances are that the coach views you as such. Therefore, you must do things to change his view. If he thinks you are the third best player, you will often get the least amount of practice time, and often the least amount of coaching.

Thus, your job is to change your own perception of what you can do, but also that of what others think you can do. The view you have of yourself may be something you are well aware of, or it can be a belief that you have that is just inherent and below your radar. The best sign is to be aware of the internal dialogue that takes place in your head. If you have low expectations for yourself, chances are you will achieve low results.

57.
It's Just A Game

"If you make every game a life and death proposition, you're going to have problems. For one thing, you'll be dead a lot."
- Dean Smith

While most of us treat sport as life and death, it clearly is not. It is not war, it is not an illness, it's just a game. Certainly the skills we develop in training, learning, preparing, and performing are traits that will help us grow as people, yet sports are simply a contest. If you lose the game, life will go on. You will certainly be upset and hopefully learn from the experience, but life will go on. If any of you have ever served in the military, been in a serious accident, had a major illness, or lost someone close to you, you will certainly know that there are many more important things in life than sports. This certainly does not mean that you don't try your best to become as good as you can, nor does it mean that you don't care deeply about the result of competition, but that losing is part of life, and it never is an excuse to drink to excess, beat your children, or injure yourself, as a result of an athletic performance.

58.
Have Faith and Confidence

"I've always believed no matter how many shots I miss,
I'm going to make the next one."
- Isiah Thomas

"My father gave me the greatest gift anyone could give
another person, he believed in me."
- Jim Valvano

"You have to be able to center yourself, to let all of your emotions go. Don't ever forget that you play with your soul as well as your body."
- Kareem Abdul-Jabbar

It is certainly one of the never-ending debates in sports. Does a person or team get confident because they do well and win or do they do well and win because they are confident? Fact is, a little of both are true. If you are a high school football team, all the confidence in the world will not beat the San Francisco 49ers. Ability and skill must be there. But in general, when teams compete on similar talent levels, confidence in coaches, teammates, and self can be all the difference. Confidence does not just happen. It is not just willed into being. It comes from dedication on all fronts. The better shape you are in, the more confident you will be as a person and team. The better and harder you practice, the more confident you will be. The more dedicated you are to the off-season training program, the more faith you will have. The harder you work, the harder it is to quit. Confidence comes from preparation. If you have given your all to prepare, then you will be confident to perform. Though it may take a while for the results to show from the work you and your team have been putting in, soon they will be there.

59.

Focus and Concentration

*"The first requisite for success is the ability to apply
your physical and mental energies to one problem
incessantly without going weary."*
- Thomas A. Edison

"We all have the ability. The difference is how we use it."
- Stevie Wonder

*"Ability is what you're capable of doing. Motivation determines what
you do. Attitude determines how well you do it."*
- Lou Holtz

The best way to convey the significance of focus and concentration is related to buying a new car. Have you noticed that when you are considering buying a new car or have just bought one, that you see every similar model on the road? Once you buy a Volkswagen Passat, you can't drive anywhere without seeing one. They are all over the place, even though you never noticed them before. If you are shopping for a house, you see every for sale sign. What your mind thinks, directly affects what you "see." Once you start to focus on specific parts of your game, you will find that improvements can quickly be made. Most people go through life without ever making any lasting change in any area because they fail to make a concentrated effort on the issue at hand.

While in the game, focus and concentration means that your sole purpose is to do the best you can at your particular role without concerning yourself with your parents, friends, girlfriends, television cameras, media, or even winning the game. If you keep yourself focused on your role, let's say covering a wide receiver, then your effort will go a long way to helping your team win the game. If your emotions cause you to leave your coverage and try to do too much, say cover someone else's man, you will hurt your team when the man you were suppose to cover is now wide open. Stay focused, do your job, be in the moment and let the rest take care of itself.

60.
Consider That Giving Up Might Be Right

"A bore is a fellow who opens his mouth and puts his feats in it."
- Henry Ford

Sports, like any endeavor will certainly have parts of it that you don't like. Even musicians who have fun and profitable careers, don't love traveling from show to show. There will be days when you won't want to practice or workout, but overall you still love participating. If you find that, for whatever reason, you are not enjoying yourself most of the time, it might be time to walk away. Whether you are in junior high or the pros, sometimes the best way to finding joy in life is stopping things you don't like doing. Shifting your focus to family, friends, studies, a job, or other hobbies, might be just the thing you need.

The only advice I offer you is to never quit during the season. If you start to play and don't like it, at least ride out the season before quitting. Often when we go to a new school, meet new people, or get a new job, we start out unhappy because we not comfortable with change. Often you will find that if you stick it out you might just find that time makes things better. However, those that quit at the first sign of unhappiness are setting themselves up for failure in other parts of life. Quitting becomes too easy. As George Costanza often said on Seinfeld, "I'm very good at quitting. I come from a long line of quitters." Reserve the right to change your mind about whatever you choose to do, but ride out that choice until the end.

61.
When Injuries Are Good

"Success is to be measured not so much by the position that one has reached in life as by the obstacles which he has overcome while trying to succeed."
- Booker T. Washington

I doubt any of you reading this book want to get hurt. In fact, we all go to great lengths to avoid it. By working out, stretching, eating right, wearing equipment, taping ankles, we take great steps to avoid injury. However, if you are to sustain a small injury, or even if you are hurt more seriously, you can gain a lot during this time. First, you may gain an appreciation for just being able to play that you may not have had before. Practices which one seemed so tough, boring, repetitious, or a waste of time, suddenly seem like the greatest thing in the world. You would give anything just to be on the field and practicing again. All the little things that previously bothered you, turn into the things which make the sport so much fun.

You can also learn to watch the game from the perspective of a coach. Since you are not concerned with your performance, you can watch with a more educational outlook. You can see things that you did not see before. You can also learn to become a better teammate. By staying involved and helping your teammates prepare and perform, even though you can't, will give you an appreciation for those who watch when you play.

Finally, it will teach you to work harder then you ever have before. Rehabbing, especially from a very serious injury will require strength and resources you never knew you had. You will have to be committed to your recovery and learn to work hard when no one is around to commend you. You will also gain a respect for the trainers and doctors who help you get back to doing what you love.

62.
You Will Miss The Camaraderie

"Even when you've played the game of your life, it's the feeling of teamwork that you'll remember. You'll forget the plays, the shots, and the scores. But you'll never forget your teammates."
- HolliesQuotes.com

Often the best way to learn is by talking to and listening to all those that have come before you. When you do, one of the overriding things that you hear from graduates, alumni, or retired players is that they miss the camaraderie of the team. The teammates that they met, practiced, trained, traveled and competed with have a special place in their hearts. It is often hard to find those types of relationships outside of sports. To have 10 or 30 or even 100 teammates that shared the same goals and went through the same experiences with you is a very special thing. You will miss your coaches, the ones who pushed you, challenged you, picked you up when you were down and motivated you when times were good. They cared for your well being off the field as well as on it.

The point is, try not to take for granted the relationships you make with teammates and coaches. They are often the ones that will be your closest throughout the rest of your life. While in the short term many of us care about our statistics, playing time, role, performance, the record of the team, most of you will be hard pressed to remember these details in twenty years. What you will remember is the work you put in with like-minded people, the joy of celebrating together, and even consoling each other. You will remember the bus rides, the car rides, the plane rides, the meetings, the trainers room, and even the time on the bench. Enjoy it all while you can, you will not soon pass this way again.

63.
Be Open Minded

"If one advances confidently in the direction of his dreams,
and endeavors to live the life which he has imagined,
he will meet with success unexpected in common hours."
- Henry David Thoreau

One of the great aspects of sports is that we often get to meet and compete with people from a variety of backgrounds, races, personalities, and appearances. A football team will have players that weigh

170 pounds and guys that weigh 350. A basketball team can have a five foot nine point guard and a seven foot center. Baseball players can be white, black, Latin, Asian, etc. Players come from all over the world with different customs, accents, and experiences. Some like to go out every night after the game, others never want to go out. The point is that athletics are often a very mixed collection of people. In so many areas of life we are around people who are exactly like us. But sports can open up that little world. Hopefully you have already learned these lessons, but it is crucial that you are open minded about the way other people choose to live. Further, you have or will learn that it is unfair to judge others until you get to know them. I have seen many times how athletes can judge opponents or new players on the team before they take the time to know them. When they do, they soon find out that they have a lot in common and can become friends.

64.
Who Are You?

"Keep on going and chances are you will stumble on something...I have never heard of anyone stumbling on something sitting down."
- Charles Kettering

"Whenever you are to do a thing, though it can never be known but to yourself, ask yourself how you would act were all the world looking at you, and act accordingly."
- Thomas Jefferson

"I expect to fight that proposition until hell freezes over. Then I propose to start fighting on the ice."
- Russell Long

Much of our culture these days seems to be about boasting who we are. Sometimes this is necessary to win a job, an election, or sell yourself to those who don't know you. To those that do know you, parents, teachers, teammates, and coaches, your actions tell of who you are. You don't need to tell your coach how much you care about winning. She can see it by your dedication to the off-season program, to showing up early for practice, by making every meeting, by getting good grades, by hustling at all times in games. In sports, our actions speak for themselves. Don't tell your teammates that you are a leader, just lead. Don't tell your coach you will get better grades, just get better grades to show him. Those that keep doing the right thing, working hard, learning the plays, growing from mistakes, and improving don't need to tell others about themselves, they are showing them. You tell the world who you are by what you do, not what you say. You cannot say you care about a class or a job assignment if you do sloppy work. If you cared, it would be done better. You cannot say you care about a meeting if you show up late, dressed sloppily. Just remember that you tell the world who you are, what your values are, and who you will become by what you do on a daily basis.

65.
Imagine Yourself As Coach

"The boss drives his men; the leader coaches them. The boss depends upon authority; the leader on good will. The boss inspires fear; the leader inspires enthusiasm. The boss says 'I' the leader 'we.' The boss fixes the blame for the breakdown; the leader fixes the breakdown. The boss says 'go;' the leader says 'let's go!'"
- H. Gordon Selfridge

"The big shots are usually the little shots who keep shooting."
- Christopher Morley

Before you are ready to rail against your coach for his practice organization, his knowledge of the game, her decision on the starting lineup, try for a moment to think about what you would do if you were the coach. If you are one of four quarterbacks and you think you

119

should be starting, try to think what it must be like for the coach to choose between the four of you. If you don't like the way the coach organizes practice, consider the other demands she might have such as a family, classes to teach, administrative duties, fundraising, radio show, recruiting, etc. While you might want your coach to be more empathetic about what it is like to be you, the fact is that almost every coach was once a player. While they may not coach with this in mind all the time, chances are that they played for a variety of coaches and know what it is like. Coaches are in the public eye and often have issues of administrators, parents, fans, boosters, and the media that you never have to face. Quite simply it is not an easy job. Your job is to perform so well that the coach has no other decision to make. If you don't like the way things are being run, ask to talk to the coach and make suggestions, he might be happy you did. Regardless of what we do in life it always helps to put ourselves in the other person's shoes. If you are a salesman, what is it like to be the one buying from you? If you are in a relationship, how does your partner feel about an issue? When you do this, you often find that you lose some of your anger because you realize that other people have views and feelings that need to be considered as well.

66.
Have Empathy For Your Opponent

*"You can make more friends in two months by becoming
interested in other people than you can in two years by
trying to get other people interested in you."*
- Dale Carnegie

*"Treat people as if they were what they out to be,
and you help them become what they are capable of being."*
- Goeth

Remember that each time you win, your opponent loses. Each time you lose, your opponent wins. This simply means that if you win a very close and exciting and important game that your opponent lost a very close and exciting and important game. You certainly deserve to celebrate and rejoice, but it will make you a better person if you can congratulate the other player or team for their effort. If a pitcher on the opposing team throws a nine inning one hitter, but that one hit was a home run that won the game 1-0 for your team, it would not kill you to tell that pitcher what a great game he pitched. That is good sportsmanship.

The same can be said if you lose. If the opposing field goal kicker makes are 57 yard kick to win the game, even though it breaks your heart, that person deserves your respect and admiration. They also deserve the right to enjoy their performance. Telling the kicker that he was "lucky and wait until next year" is poor sportsmanship. You should always be graceful in defeat. You will be a better person if you walk up and tell him what a great kick it was and that he could kick for your team any day. Next time you play them, do what you can so that he does not have a chance to win the game in the last seconds.

67.
Be Low Maintenance

"There ain't no man can avoid being born average.
But there ain't no man got to be common."
- Satchel Paige

"I think and think for months and years. Ninety-nine times,
the conclusion is false. The hundredth time I am right."
- Albert Einstein

Those of you that saw the movie When Harry Met Sally surely remember the scene where Billy Crystal explains to Meg Ryan that she is high maintenance. Instead of just ordering a salad and letting it go at that, she has about 85 rules for how the salad should be prepared. By the time she is done ordering, the waitress wants to quit her job. This is not the type of person and player you ever want to become. High maintenance athletes have an issue with everything. They don't like the uniform, they need to get a special number, they have to sit in a certain seat during a meeting or on a bus trip. They are a problem in class, they show up late to practice, they don't know the plays. The more a coach has to be concerned with you carrying out every one of her assignments or rules, the more trouble you are to them. Even if you are a stellar athlete, this will soon wear thin on your teammates and coaches. Low maintenance players don't show up late, they are a half hour early. They don't care what their number is, what the uniform color is, they just want a jersey and to play. They attend class, if they need to make an appearance they do it, they know the signs, they know the plays. Those players eventually rise to the top because they will be ready for the opportunity when it comes their way. When the time comes that they need the help of a teammate or coach for something unrelated to the team or sport, others are willing to help. This certainly doesn't mean that you don't have issues or problems it is just that you are not a constant source of headaches for others.

68.

It Only Takes You To Practice

"What counts is not the number of hours you put in,
but how much you put in the hours."
- Anonymous

"I feel that the greatest reward for doing
is the opportunity to do more."
- Dr. Jonas Salk

There is no denying the fact that we often need a team or at least several people to be able to practice many of our skills properly. But with the proper motivation, some equipment, and often a little bit of creativity we can improve a great deal on our own. I am not referring to working out or running, but actually practicing sport specific skills. In baseball or softball you can throw a ball against a wall and field the return throw. You can hit yourself fly balls with a tennis ball and a racket. You can hit off a tee or a machine. In basketball you can shoot and dribble all day. In lacrosse, soccer, field and ice hockey you can shoot as well. In tennis you can serve or use a machine, for volleyball you can work on your serve. In all but a few sports you can really work on key skills by yourself. Add in one more person and you can cover almost all the skills you would need in your sport. Many athletes simply come to practice at the specified times and leave when it is over. If you have been assigned a tough workout, this should be enough. If not, you need to take it upon yourself to work harder. If you arrive at practice early, instead of waiting for teammates to come out, work on your own particular weaknesses. If you are there with another player, instead of simply talking to kill time, work on something worthwhile. If you are in high school or college, you have lots of restrictions on your practice time and therefore need to work more on your own or with a few other teammates if you want to improve. A two hour softball practice where you spend an hour of it standing around leaves a great deal of work to be done. Especially when you consider that individual sport athletes, such as tennis players, golfers, skaters, and gymnasts, will work on their sport for five or more grueling hours a day. If you are a shortstop on the softball team you really need a hundred ground balls a day, 50 pop ups, and 100 swings a day. You might never get that in a team practice where the coach has many players to concentrate on and a full team with which she has to be concerned.

69.
Discipline and Sacrifice

"He banged the door on the way out, and out of that
bang came eventually the Chrysler Corporation."
- Alfred P. Sloan, Jr.
on Walter Chrysler's departure from General Motors

Noting comes easy in life. If it does, chances are you will pay for what you received in other ways. While it is my hope that you find the road to your goals to be enjoyable in each step, the fact of the matter remains that there will be sacrifice along the way. For every doctor that you know who is making a great living, there was a great deal of discipline and sacrifice that went into getting good grades in college and on medical school entrance exams. There is sacrifice of giving up most outside activities while in medical school. There is much discipline required to do the work while in school. The end payoff is worth it to those that make it through - a well paying, prestigious career in which they help others in the process. But make no mistake, the road is not an easy one. The same goes for any athletic goal. Being your best, winning games, winning championships, losing weight, increasing your strength or speed, all take a tremendous amount of discipline and sacrifice. Where others might go to Florida at spring break time, you might drive to Arizona to find the speed training guru who increases your speed by 10%. When others eat and drink what they want, you refrain. To become what you always wanted to be, you need to live a different life then the average person. You will not sleep late, eat fast food, drink soda or coffee, skip workouts, or have 10 different hobbies. Rather you will have a goal of becoming the best you can at whatever you endeavor and you will take pride in making the sacrifices for your goals. You will learn to delay gratification. You will not react to your every whim; rather you will have a greater purpose in all that you do.

70.
Bored Means Not Enough Goals

"Of all the unhappy people in the world, the unhappiest
are those who have not found something they want to do.
True happiness comes to him who does his work well,
followed by a relaxing and refreshing period of rest. True
happiness comes from the right amount of work for the day."
- Lin Yutang

"If you're bored with life - you don't get up every morning with a burning desire to do things - you don't have enough goals"
- Lou Holtz

If you are bored with life, chances are you have not set up enough goals to challenge yourself. If you sleep a lot, play solitaire on the computer, watch mindless television, or play video games on a regular basis, or simply find that life is often too boring, you may want to look at things in a different way. This is not to say that every once in a while you don't get to take it easy. At times we all need to zone out. However, if this happens too often, consider this. Would you be as bored with life if you tried to learn something new? What if you decided to learn to play the guitar? How much fun would it be to take lessons, buy a book, a video, a CD and teach yourself how to play? It doesn't mean you have to become the next Eddie Van Halen, just that you would get endless hours of pleasure learning to play songs you like to listen to. If you get good enough you could play for friends, at parties, camping, for your girlfriend or boyfriend, one day for your kids. Maybe even start a little band eventually.

If music is not your thing, how about trying to write an article, book, or movie? Maybe you just start to read the classic novels or watch the classic movies. You could also try to learn another sport or even another position within your sport. You could read books or watch videos about your sport so that you learn as much as possible about the game. The fact is, if you sleep to noon every day, you simply have not set goals. Depending on the way you look at life, it can be filled with so much to do and learn and see or it can simply be boring, whereby you wait for others to provide fun and excitement or turn to other things, such as drugs, to avoid facing life. The choice is yours.

71.
Preparation

"The dictionary is the only place where success comes before work."
- Arthur Brisbane

"Most people have the will to win, few have the will to prepare."
- Bobby Knight

Know anyone who doesn't want to win? Really, do you know someone who would rather lose then win? I doubt it. We all want to win, that is often our motivation for playing. While the joy in sport comes from simply playing the game, few play to lose. Yet, as much as we all want to win, few have the will to prepare. Tiger Woods has been known to hit balls on the range and lift weights after a grueling round. When others would immediately be with friends or family, or have a meal and a drink, Tiger would still have work to do after he got off the course. Nolan Ryan would ride the stationary bike forty-five minutes after each outing. He did this because it would help his arm recover and get him ready for his next start. He did it when he won and when he lost, when he pitched well and when he didn't. How good would an army be without training? Could a marathon be run without training? Can a pitcher throw 100 pitches without training? Can a basketball player play forty minutes without training? The higher the level you compete often means the more preparation that has to be done. While a high school football coach may have videotape of his upcoming opponent and show it to his quarterback, the professional quarterback has at his fingertips, every single play the upcoming opponents defense has run all year. There is much preparation to be done in the gym, on the practice floor, and in the video room.

72.

Commitment

*"Look around and you'll agree that the really happy people
are those who have broken the chains of procrastination,
those who find satisfaction in doing the job at hand.
They're full of eagerness, zest, productivity. You can be, too.*
- Norman Vincent Peale

"The harder you work, the harder it is to quit."
- Vince Lombardi

*"The quality of a person's life is in direct proportion
to their commitment to excellence, regardless of their
chosen field of endeavor."*
- Vince Lombardi

Simply put, you are either in or out, there is no in between. You are
with us or against us. This commitment comes in several forms. First
you owe it to yourself to be committed to any endeavor you under-
take. Just to be involved in something without caring about the
results is a recipe for poor results in life. You certainly don't have to

be 100% committed to all that you do, but for those things that you claim matter to you, it needs to be all or nothing. You cannot just be committed to the good times, the victories, the games, you need to be committed to the practice, the workouts, and the improvement. Taken a step further you owe it to your teammates to be committed. Whenever you accept being part of a group, you need to put in your share of work and effort. If the entire team is marching toward a long term goal, but you don't really care about whether or not it is achieved, you should consider getting out. The fact is, sooner or later your team will need to depend on you and it is unfair to let them down. This does not mean you will come through in every key situation, but more importantly that you gave it your all in preparing and performing. If you are committed all the way and don't get the desired result, your teammates will support you. In addition, you owe commitment to all those that support your effort. Coaches, parents, administrators, fans, etc. While you should never play the game for others, you certainly do owe them your best effort. Coaches have committed to working with you, your parents have given in many ways to support your athletic career, administrators have worked a great deal to organize, schedule, fundraise, equip, and promote your efforts. Fans support you with their time, energy, and money. To these people you owe nothing but your best effort.

73.

Pressure

*"Pressure is something you feel
when you don't know what you're doing."*
- Chuck Noll

Pick your favorite topic and think about giving a speech on it. If you know about growing tomatoes, think about giving a speech on that. Might be a little pressure, standing up in front of others, but you will most likely make it through just fine, since you know your subject well. Now imagine giving a speech about the details of the 7/10 split in bowling, even though you don't know a thing about bowling. Think that's a little more pressure? Should be. The more you know about what you are doing, the more confident you are doing it and the less pressure you will feel.

The more you learn about what you are doing in your sport, the less pressure you will feel doing it. In turn, the more you can practice what you need to do, the less pressure you will feel doing it. When casual golfers play with friends, short puts are often missed when there is money on the line. A putt which normally would be easy to knock in, now looks like trouble. If the golfer wants to feel less pressure in that situation, she could go to the practice range and sink short putts for an hour a week. That will give her a lot more confidence in making those putts in the future. When you take the final exam for a class, there is plenty of pressure if you haven't studied enough and don't know the subject matter. You begin to feel pressure as soon as you come to a question you don't know. Then you begin to put even more pressure on yourself because you know that a bad grade on the final will mean a bad grade for the course. This leads you to think that if you fail the course you will not get credit for it and have to repeat it. You will have to explain why you failed to your teacher, counselor, and parents. The pressure builds. If you know the subject matter very well, the test becomes a fun challenge and one you feel confident taking. When my wife gave birth to our son, we felt the pressure since we had never had the experience before. The doctor, who had delivered thousands of babies, was calm throughout. She had done it many times before. I imagine if she had to deliver the baby on an airplane, or in the hospital when complications ensued, she would feel more pressure.

If you struggle to throw strikes during any given situation when you are pitching, then you will feel a tremendous amount of pressure pitching with the bases loaded. Yet if you have excellent control, then you feel ready for the challenge, not just preoccupied with not walking the batter.

Again, pressure is felt more by those who are unprepared. If prepared, the right pressure can bring your performance to a whole new level.

74.
It's Never Over

"It ain't over, til it's over."
- Yogi Berra

If there is any major lesson to be learned through athletics, none can be much higher then to learn that it is never over. The game, the season, your career, is not completely over until there is no game left to play. Yogi's quote is very true. You are never out of any game until the last out, the final seconds, the last point, or final swing are over. You lose only when you give up. Even if you have lost when the game is over because the score shows you are behind, you are still a winner if you gave everything you had until the end. Be the person who plays hard until the end and rallies the others to do so as well.

If you were in a platoon in the army would you consider the battle over if half your men had been injured or killed or would you fight until the bitter end? The same holds true in any athletic contest. If the other person or team takes an early lead the game is only over if you feel that it is. Even if they continue to beat you, if you compete as hard as you can until the true end, you will gain respect, and teach yourself the key lesson of life. Be aware of your body language and your effort level. Those that give up do so because they believe that they have no chance to come back and win. Never allow this frame of mind. Just continue to work and play as hard as you can until the referee or umpire tells you the game is over.

The same can be said for any season. While every athlete, coach, and team wants to win every game and as many games as possible, no season is over until all the games have been played. I have told all my teams over my career, those that had a great record and those that did not, to play each game as hard as they can and it will be my job to tell them when the next one is. In other words, when players begin to think about how many wins they need for a playoff, or a school record, or to reach .500, or worse they are concerned about the record for the other team then problems ensue. Just play every game on the schedule as hard as you can and if you make the play-offs, the coach will tell you when and where to show up. Once in the playoffs, play hard as you can for as long as you can and the coach will tell you if there are more games or not.

75.
Consistency

"If I miss one day's practice, I notice it. If I miss two days, the critics notice it. If I miss three days, the audience notices."
- Ignace Paderewski (pianist)

"It's hard to motivate rich football players."
- Bill Parcells

Many athletes can have a moment when they shine. While a one time great moment is better then no moment at all, consistency is more important then anything else in an athletic career. From a coaching perspective, most would rather have players who give a solid, reliable performance on a regular basis then the one who is capable of both a great or horrific game each time they play. Consistency is obtained primarily through constant dedication to hard work and improvement. Once an athlete rests, the results will falter. For the marathoner, training for one race does not mean you stop running if you plan to run future races. Even if the race is won, there are more to run and more to win. Win and work hard. Lose and work hard. Tie and work hard. When the season is over, work hard. In the pre-season, work hard. Do not allow yourself to fall into the frame of mind where good results means less work. All the famous athletes that have lasted a long time at the professional level embody this principal. They never let their success make them soft. Rather they motivate themselves to stay at their level or performance or even improve.

76.
Belief

"Confidence is contagious. So is lack of confidence."
- Michael O'Brien

"Our belief at the beginning of a doubtful undertaking is the one thing that insures the successful outcome of our venture.
- William James

Right now, change you life. Right now, change your attitude. Right now, start committing yourself to believing in everything that you want. If you got cut from the team, know that when you work hard you will make it next season. Right now, know that though you were not a starter last year that you are a great player and deserve to start every game. Right now, eliminate every negative thought that enters your head. Right now know that your coach is the perfect person to help you achieve your goals. Right now, know deep in your heart that your upbringing and your family life have put you in perfect position to be an elite athlete and to achieve your goals. Right now, know that you can take five more strokes off your game, you can throw five miles an hour harder, you can lift more weight then ever before, run faster, and out smart your opponent. Right now, believe that you will find a way to improve, that you have it in you to achieve great things. Right now, know that you will win. Right now, know that you will no longer stand for anything other then your best performance. Eliminate all thoughts that don't lead to your goal. Believe in yourself, you are the only you that you will ever be. Believe in your parents, they are the only ones you will ever have. Believe in our teammates, for this season they will not change. If you can first change your attitude to a positive frame of mind, even in the face of trouble or adversity, you will be on to a much better athletic and life experience.

77.
Be Mindful

"Time is the only capital that any human being has,
and the only thing he can't afford to lose."
- Thomas Edison

"You can see a lot by observing."
- Yogi Berra

Being more mindful will assist you in any area of life, not just athletics. The fact is that most of us often go through the motions in many parts of our lives. Take driving for example. Even though we are operating an expensive machine at high speeds with dangers all around us, many of us drive while on cell phones, talking to others, reaching into the back seat, or simply not paying attention to the road. Often we can drive for a period of time and when we think about the details of the trip, are hard pressed to remember any of it. Much is the same way we go through various aspects of life - asleep. Even though we are awake, we are on automatic pilot. In terms of athletics this can harm your career. I have often seen individuals or teams practicing and it is interesting to watch those who simply go through the motions, such as when they are doing a drill they don't want to do. Every time we practice we have an opportunity to get better, if we pay attention to what we are doing. The golfer who goes to the driving range and hits ball after ball without thought or purpose might be warming up muscles, but certainly not learning. Working on your golf swing means being aware of the subtle changes in your swing and how they affect the golf ball. Such practice can carry over to actual competition. Regardless of the sport, being mindful in a game means that you are completely mentally aware of the situation and your role. Instead of being surprised by the actions of your opponent, you anticipate what they might do. Most great players have this gift. While physical gifts are very important, being mentally alert at all times can make you the type of player who always seems to make the right play, be in the right place, and make all the right decisions. Those kinds of players will always be in the game.

78.

Somewhere

*"Inventors and men of genius have almost always been regarded
as fools at the beginning of their careers."*
- Dostoevsky

Life is full of choices. Somewhere in the world at this very instant someone is: dying, being born, crying, laughing, working, sleeping, jogging, smoking for the first time, smoking for the last time, trying drugs for the first time, going into rehab, taking drugs for the last time, getting married, getting divorced, making love, fighting, being overwhelmed by life, finding great joy in life, working out, being a couch potato, lifting weights, lifting dessert, committing a crime, stopping a crime, helping others, hurting others, being honest, lying, driving drunk, taking the keys from a drunk who wants to drive, trying to live forever, committing suicide, overeating, dying of hunger, helping the environment, dumping waste, building a home, becoming homeless, finding the joy in hard work, finding a way to avoid hard work, learning a new skill, being bored with life, playing a sport, practicing, meditating, stressing out, doing what needs to be done, procrastinating, doing homework, and playing video games. It is up to you to decide who you want to be and what you will become for the limited time we all get the gift of being alive on this planet. Choose wisely.

79.
The Big Picture

"Let every nation know, whether it wishes us well or ill,
that we shall pay any price, bear any burden, meet any hardship,
support any friend, oppose any foe to assure the survival
and the success of liberty."
- John F. Kennedy

Part of becoming a mature person entails understanding that life is an amazing gift, not something to be taken for granted. When you take time to really contemplate life, you can't help but feel less frustrated by the little things. Traffic suddenly doesn't seem so bad when you realize that life is a blessing, a scientific accident. It does not exist anywhere else that we know. Next time you feel that you have big problems, take a look at a globe, the stars, sun or moon and see if what you consider so big continues to feel that way. I don't mean to say that watching the stars will pay off your student loan. In fact I can guarantee it won't. What it will do is to make you realize that having the problem of a loan is much better then some of the alternatives. That in the big picture, you'd rather be alive, facing and overcoming life's issues, then the alternative, which is no life at all.

Want the history of the world in few words? Here goes. 15 billion years ago the Big Bang. First the universe was small and hot and over time it began to cool and expand. Over millions of years atomic particles of hydrogen and helium gas produced stars, galaxies, planets, and eventually people. 10 billion years later our solar system is formed. Here are some facts that should amaze you or make your head hurt. Maybe both. Our galaxy, the Milky Way, has about 200 billion stars. There are about 100 billion galaxies in the universe. The most distant objects modern science can detect are 87,000 million million million miles away. Far enough to make the plane ride to Australia seem a bit more manageable. Out of all this, Earth is the only place that we know of that has life. That is perspective.

Here's more. The earliest detection of human life began about 3.5 million years ago. Humans have been a part of the universe for only .023% of its existence. The amount of time you and I will spend on the planet compared to the history of the universe is so small it won't register on a calculator. This is something you might want to keep in mind the next time the toll gate doesn't go up, even though you put in the right amount of change.

When you are not sure about what you really want to do for work, if you will ever find the right person, or any other issue that constantly plagues you, just realize that as bad as life can seemingly get, it still is a gift each and every day that you wake up. Open this gift of life and today make yourself a better athlete and person. Play with gusto, with passion, with pride.

80.
You Can Be

"Genius is one percent inspiration and 99 percent perspiration."
- Thomas Edison

You can be almost anything you want. While some things can be out of reach, President of the United States, music star, famous actor, world's richest person, most of what you desire can be had if you simply choose a goal and then constantly work towards it. Don't allow others to negatively influence your life's path. More importantly, don't allow yourself to do so. No matter where you are in life right now, if you decided to become a doctor, you can do it. While it might be a long road academically, financially, intellectually, and chronologically, it can be done. Whether you read this as a high school student with a D average or a fifty year old secretary who hates her job, you can become a doctor. It might be impossible to become a pro athlete but you can certainly become the best athlete you can be. You can master your sport at your talent level. You can learn a new sport or position. You might not win the New York City marathon, but you can become one who finishes it. One armed men have played Major League Baseball. Legally blind players have played in the National Football League. There are many blind skiers and golfers. You can do what you set your mind to. You can be what you want to be.

81.
Go Watch Kids

"Anything worth doing is worth doing poorly
until you learn to do it well."
- Steve Brown

*"Continuous effort, not strength or intelligence
is the key to unlocking our potential."*
- Liane Cordes

*"Better to be driven out from among men
than to be disliked of children."*
- Richard H. Dana

It is certainly true that watching any highly skilled performance can motivate you. In fact, one time while simply channel surfing I was so motivated by watching a man juggle many (at least 10) plastic balls with his mouth that I got right off the couch and went for a run. If you are a shortstop, going to Yankee Stadium to watch Derek Jeter is a great source of inspiration.

What I have also found is motivating is watching kids play. Watching five and six year old soccer, baseball, basketball, football, or lacrosse players, any sport for that matter, is wonderful. It is truly the grass roots level of sports. It is not about the money, ego, even victory. It's simply about playing. In the moment, sheer joy, running around, not in school, not doing homework, not eating veggies, outright athletic bliss. If you ever find that your sport is becoming work or that you are losing the joy you once had, go watch the little kids play. Then remind yourself, you too are still a little kid, just in a bigger body.

82.

There Is No Offseason

"You must see your goals clearly and specifically
before you can set out for them. Hold them in your mind
until they become second nature."
¬- Les Brown

"If at first you don't succeed, try, try, try again."
- William E. Hickson

Regardless of your age or talent level, it is important that you understand athletics are a full time endeavor. If you are not playing, you
are preparing to play. If you are not in formal practice, you are lifting weights and conditioning. If you play two or three sports, you
are always in season. To become a quality athlete, you need to think
of your sport in much grander terms then simply the playing season.
How good would Eric Clapton be if he played guitar three months
a year when he was first learning? I don't mean that you overdue it
to the point of burnout, but that you realize that to become your
best at anything, it takes a full time commitment. When one starts
a company, do you think they work the typical forty-hours? Not a

chance. It takes long days to make any venture a success. Imagine trying to lose weight by eating well three days a week, but horribly on the other four. To compete at the of highest of levels requires a full-time effort. If you practice or play simply when you feel like it, that is a hobby, not a complete dedication to the sport. There is nothing wrong with having hobbies, but it you treat your main sport as such, don't be surprised or upset when you don't achieve the results you were seeking. If you don't make a full commitment to whatever it is that you do, you will soon find that the others who are will pass you right by.

83.
What Will Your Legacy Be?

"The measure of a man's real character is what
he would do if he knew he would never be found out."
- Thomas Macaulay

"The time to repair the roof is when the sun is shining."
- John F. Kennedy

Have you ever stopped to consider how you might be remembered? Will you be a person who starts a dynasty for your team? Will you turn around a losing program? Will you continue the winning ways for a successful club? Will you be a record holder? A coach's favorite? Will you be a player the team talks about in years to come? Will your number be retired? Will you be a success story that the coach tells to future players in the program? Or will you be the guy who played half a season and quit for a job at Wendy's? Will you get frustrated at the coach and blame him for your situation? Are you the type of girl who expects the starting job she now has, to always be hers? Or will you be the type who works so hard that no matter who comes onto the team, you will always have your place? Will you rely on your natural talent or work to bring out the very best that you can be? If you aren't going to be remembered for the number of points scored, how about for the hustle you showed on the floor? If you are not the girl who hit the school record for home runs, why not be the one who ran full speed to first every single time? Maybe you won't lead the team in goals scored, but you were the one who got in front of the puck on every opponent's shot. Maybe you didn't start every game, but you did all you could to bring out the best in your teammates. You tell the world, each and every day, who you are by your actions. Do you let adversity bring you down or make you stronger? When the other team went up by two early touchdowns, did you know in your heart that there was no chance to win or did you just play each play as hard as you possibly could and just let the results take care of themselves?

84.

How Are You Motivated?

*"Few men during their lifetime come anywhere
near exhausting the resources dwelling within them.
There are deep wells of strength that are never used."*
- Admiral Richard Byrd

While this book and others like it can help give you some thoughts
and ideas about ways to keep you motivated and focused to reach
your goals, it is important that you understand what drives you.
What works for one might not for another. If you are a junior high
school athlete, your goal might simply be to make a team and have
fun at your sport. If you are a college athlete, your goal might be to
play professionally. If you are a stockbroker just starting a workout
program, your goal may simply be to get in better shape to improve
the quality of your life. We all have different goals and different reasons for reaching them. What is important is that if you are looking
for a way to increase your effort, you need to be your own counselor.
What motivates you? What is your incentive? How can you reward
yourself when you reach your goal? You might hate to jog on your
own, but would love to do it with your wife. If she doesn't want to
run, just the thought of having her ride a bike while you run, so you

both can be together might simply be the trick to getting you moving and changing the way you look and feel. Maybe music will help. Prayer, a support group, or visualization. Coach yourself, take notes, keep a journal. Remember, in this world NO ONE cares more about you then you.

85.
Parents

"The hardest part of raising children is teaching them to ride bicycles. A father can run beside the bicycle or stand yelling directions while the child falls. A shaky child on a bicycle for the first time needs both support and freedom. The realization that this is what the child will always need can hit hard."
- Sloan Wilson

"If you want your children to keep their feet on the ground, put some responsibility on their shoulders."
- Abigail Van Buren

"Children need models more than they need critics."
- Joseph Joubert

In my years of coaching I have learned a great deal about how parenting affects people. For the most part, the athletes I coached that come from a good family support system are those that do well academically, are goal oriented and motivated, easy to coach, and socially well adjusted. Those who have various issues from their home life seem to require a great deal of parenting in college. They miss class, skip practice without calling, have few goals, have no idea what they might want to do after college, and given the chance, their favorite pastime is to sleep. Out of all the counseling on all the issues I have done in my coaching career, the one that I find hardest to understand and thus advise is that athlete/person who has few goals. I am always shocked when I ask an athlete what drives and motivates them in life and their answer is "I don't know" or "nothing." This can be traced back to parenting.

If you are a parent, the best thing you can give your child is unconditional love. Those parents who are disinterested in their children's athletic accomplishments will lead to problems. Just the same I have seen many parents who are frustrated athletes who put entirely too much pressure on their kids as a result of their own failed career. Kids don't need that type of pressure and they don't want to be told what to do just because you say so. They want to be motivated in a more positive way. If you want your kid to workout more, why don't you workout with them? If you want them to run, go for a run with them. Play catch, shoot baskets, hit balls, etc. In addition, the sooner you can teach your kids to fight their own battles on their team, the better off they will be. You will not be calling their bosses if there is a problem at work one day, nor will you call their spouse, so when possible, avoid calling the coach. If there is a legitimate issue, have your child set up a meeting with the coach. If they don't feel comfortable you can be in the meeting. But if you take the matter solely into your hands, you are retarding the development of your child. I am certainly not an expert on child rearing, I just know what I see. As I recruit and meet so many kids, I can quickly see that the apple does not fall far from the tree.

As children, we also need to understand that our parents are doing the best they can. Sometimes this is good enough, other times it is not. Soon we all need to grow up enough to hear and care what they think, but to make our own decisions in life.

86.
Learn To Switch Moods/Modes

"No vision and you perish; No Ideal, and you're lost;
Your heart must ever cherish Some faith at any cost.
Some hope, some dream to cling to, Some rainbow in the
sky, Some melody to sing to, Some service that is high."
- Harriet Du Autermont

Your ability to be a different person at different times is important in life and key in athletics. While it is not necessary to act like the others around you, it is important in life that you adapt to your situation. For example, if you are playing poker with your friends, it would be expected that the conversation is a little different, then if you are meeting your girlfriend's parents for the first time. You talk differently to co-workers you have known for years then you would on a job interview. And such is life. While we are at the core the same person, we present a different part of ourselves based on the environment we are in at the moment.

Much is the same in athletics. Your mood would be different if you are in the game playing with intensity as compared to being on the bench, calmly waiting for your next opportunity. In the locker room before the game you are building a quiet intensity, yet after the game you appreciatively shake hands with your opponent, talk to the media, and meet your friends and family with a different attitude. The way you are in class or at a job, with your girlfriend, your friends, and when you practice and play, all should bring out a different side of who you are. Often bringing the different sides of your personality to the wrong place can mean trouble. If you take your game day attitude toward your teacher, you might be in some trouble. Just the same way you don't want to be the nice boyfriend on the football field. Your job there is to be intense and physically and mentally dominate your opponent. You don't want to hurt them, and you will shake hands after, but during the game, you are not looking to be nice, but to be the intense competitor that helps you achieve your peak performance.

87.

Each Day You Can Be Reborn

"The great thing in the world is not so much where we stand, as in what direction we are moving."
- Oliver Wendell Holmes

"Guts are a combination of confidence, courage, conviction, strength of character, stick-to-itiveness, pugnaciousness, backbone, and intestinal fortitude. They are mandatory for anyone who wants to get to and stay at the top."
- D.A. Benton

"Write it on your heart that every day is the best day in the year. He or she is rich who owns the day and no one owns the day who allows it to be invaded with threat and anxiety. Finish every day and be done with it. You have done what you could. Some blunders and absurdities no doubt crept in. Forget them as soon as you can. Tomorrow is a new day. Begin it well and serenely with too high a spirit to be encumbered with your old nonsense. This new day is too clear, with its hopes and invitations, to waste a moment on the yesterdays."
- Ralph Waldo Emerson

We all make New Year's resolutions, yet very few of them stick. The reason seems to be, more then any other, that it is not easy to make complete change just because the calendar says it is a new year. Changing simply based on the fact that a new year is upon us, is not enough incentive to make lasting change.

The fact is that each day of your life is a brand new day and one that allows you to make of it what you want. Each day you have the chance to make the change that you want, to exchange bad habits for good, to commit yourself to your goals, to do whatever it is that you want. Each day is the first day in the remainder of your athletic career. Each day is the first day in the rest of your life. Do not get caught up in yesterday which is now out of your control. If yesterday you did not start that walking plan you wanted to, today you can. If you do not do it today, then you can start tomorrow. You do not have to wake up tomorrow morning the same person who goes to bed tonight.

88.
Be Proactive

*"Become a possibilitarian. No matter how dark things seem
to be or actually are, raise your sights and see possibilities -
always see them, for they're always there."*
- Norman Vincent Peale

"It is better to wear out than to rust out."
- Richard Cumberland

"If you don't run your own life, somebody else will."
- John Atkinson

This is an issue I often see in the world of work, but it certainly relates to athletics and all areas of life as well. Those who have successful careers usually are those that created their situation. Instead of sitting back and waiting for an employer to call or using an employment agency to look for jobs or just simply mass mailing resumes, those who have good careers worked hard to get them. They networked and met new people, went to job fairs, perfected the skill of the informational interview, and generally did everything they could to put themselves in a position to get the kind of job that would be rewarding, as opposed to simply getting the job that is easiest to get. Very often you will hear people complain about the economy or the job market and while these may have some bearing depending on the type of work you seek, plenty of people are getting hired regardless of the economic conditions. The reason is that companies always need good people.

Much can be related to the world of athletics. The athletes that wind up doing the best are often those that seek out new ways to improve, learn, and better themselves. Instead of waiting for the right coaching to come along, they go find it. If there is no one able near you able to help with your strength training, instead of just giving up on working out, you will read books or seek out experts to get the information. If your school doesn't have a gym, then join one. If that is not possible, do pushups, sit ups, pull ups, and plyometrics to gain strength.

Often in life if you simply sit back and wait for the right help, job, relationship, etc. to come along, you might find yourself waiting a long time. Then out of desperation, you might just take the easiest thing you can get. Instead go after what you want.

89.
Self-Image

"The art of being yourself at your best is the art of
unfolding your personality into the man you want to be...
Be gentle with yourself, learn to love yourself, to forgive yourself,
for only as we have the right attitude toward ourselves can
we have the right attitude toward others.
- Wilfred Peterson

Any sports psychologist will tell you that much of your performance relates to your self-image. Those with low self-esteem will have a hard time showing their true potential. The type of self-image I am referring to is both on and off the athletic field. While some athletes can have a poor self-image outside their sport but have a good one within it, most often the two relate. Self-image is several things, most importantly it is accepting yourself as you are. We spend much of our lives comparing ourselves to our peers - whether it be looks, money, clothes, etc., we often feel that we need to match up to be worthy. However, while we all want to fit in on some level, we certainly would not want a world where everyone is alike. Life is interesting because people are different and unique. No one else has your experience, your skills, and your personality. Further, we all too often make the mistake of assuming that others have a great life as we view them from the outside. But even kings have their troubles. You are better off not trying to judge others about how happy or unhappy they might be. Better just do the best job you can of being yourself and improving what you can. When it comes to your sport, you will find that the more you practice, the more you learn, and the better you get, will directly turn into an improved image while playing and lead to much better results.

90.
Quality vs. Quantity

"I learned the value of hard work by working hard."
- Margaret M. Fitzpatrick

I am very fortunate to have been able to work with a variety of youths in a variety of sports. For the most part it is so great to watch them play, they bring a simple joy to the sport that most would benefit from watching. However, if you watch them practice, it is often another story. The biggest mistake young kids make, and often the rest of us as well, is that we confuse quantity with quality. What your average eight year old will do when told to shoot free throws is put up about 30 shots in a minute (assuming they can chase down the ball that fast). Instead of working on any specific technique, they just fire up shots and think that that counts as good practice. I have seen teenagers hit baseballs off a batting tee so fast that you can actually see sweat coming off their heads while they get out of breath. When was the last time you saw a batter in a game get tired at the plate?

The point is that when we are practicing, especially when learning a new skill, you must take your time. Nothing can be learned if you do it a hundred miles an hour. When going that fast it is hard to concentrate on any technique. If you play golf, you will know that often when you miss a putt or hit a bad shot, it is because you rushed.

Doing five excellent repetitions of whatever you are working on is much better then doing 25 with poor technique. This is especially true when working out with weights. So many of us want to do the heaviest weight possible for as many repetitions as we can, without concerning ourselves with proper form. Certainly going to the weight room and doing things wrong is still better then not going at all, but the way to get the best results is with the right form. First pick the proper weight. You will find that if you do any movement with both good form and concentration on the negative aspect, you will be using less weight then if you did the exercise much faster. Once you have the right weight, take time doing the exercise. Breath in with each negative and then out with each positive. Use a full range of motion and control the weight on both phases of the lift. Using momentum to move the weights around might make you feel stronger, but you are not getting anywhere near the gains you could be getting with proper form.

When learning any new skill, start at a very slow speed. Try slow motion if necessary, then as you learn gradually increase speed. Doing it right is much more important then doing it quickly. Emphasize quality over quantity. I'd rather have one Porsche then five beat up cars.

91.
Make Memories and Moments

"We do not remember days, we remember moments."
- Cesare Pavese

When most athletes look back on their careers, they remember the moments. The moments during practice where something funny occurred. In games, we remember many of the big moments rather then the specifics of a full game. I played college athletics and can hardly remember anything related to the record of our teams or my personal statistics. What I do remember are the friendships I made, the big games we played, the fun we had riding on the bus. Granted I did not play at the premier level where national championship games were played before hundreds of thousands in the stands and millions on television, but it was still college athletics. The point is, what you will remember years from now are the moments when you achieved as a team, when you made lifelong friends, and other details outside of just wins and losses. Make moments today.

92.
Potential

"The greatest waste in the world is the difference between what we are and what we could become."
- Ben Herbster

"Most people live, whether physically, intellectually or morally, in a very restricted circle of their potential being. They make very small use of their possible consciousness, and of their soul's resources in general, much like a man who, out of his whole bodily organism, should get into a habit of using and moving only his little finger."
- William James

I am not a big believer in potential. That fact is that all of us could be much better in a particular area of our lives if we set our minds to it. I am a very poor guitar player. I enjoy just teaching myself and playing a little for relaxation. I am sure I have the potential to become an excellent guitar player. It would simply take two lessons a week, three hours of practice a day, for about three years. However, since I have so many other things going on in my life, I chose not to commit my time to achieving my guitar-playing peak. I lose no sleep over my choice and will not, thirty years from now, look back and say that I should have been a professional guitarist.

I do, however, have some regrets about my athletic career. I believe that if I was pushed a little bit more by others, and a whole lot more by myself, I could have been a much better athlete. If only I knew then what I know now. For those of you who have a career fully ahead of you, or are even in the midst of one, you should have no other goal then to work as hard as you can at your sport until the time comes when you can't play any longer. If you have given it your all and you have enough talent, then hopefully you can play your sport for a living. If not, you will at least be able to rest and pursue other things in life knowing that you gave all you could.

93.
You Are Not Owed Anything

"You put together the best team that you can with the players you've got, and replace those who aren't good enough."
- Robert Crandall

Just because you were a starter last year, does not mean you have to be a starter this year. If you are on scholarship as a college athlete, it does not mean you cannot be beaten out for your position by a walk on. If you signed a big contract last year, it doesn't mean you get your spot automatically. The moment you begin to feel that you are owed anything in your career, you are in trouble. Sure, you can expect some loyalty for your hard work and service to a team or program, but it does not mean that you do not have to do your part to keep up. As a coach, I try to be as honest as possible with my players. Even if that means telling them exactly what they have to do to make the team next season or not lose their spot by an incoming freshman. Complacency kills careers. Don't let it happen to you.

The same goes in almost all walks of life. Your spouse does not owe you anything. Just because you were nice to her years ago, but now you don't treat her well, she doesn't owe it to stay married to you. Sure you had a great year on the job last year, but this year you are showing up late, unprepared, and not doing the same quality work as in the past. The boss and the company will certainly give you time and chances to improve, especially if you are having personal problems, but at some point, they simply need a person in place to do the work. They don't owe you a job or your salary. It is certainly fine to be in an environment where you need to prove yourself every minute of every day, but a the same time past performance is great but just that, in the past. Don't expect to be owed anything because in most situations in life, if you don't perform you can be replaced.

94.
Read

"In the case of good books, the point is not how many of them you can get through, but rather how many can get through to you."
- Mortimer J. Adler

If I were asked for one suggestion on the best way an athlete can improve his or her career, it would be to read. Depending on what you read, it can provide you with inspiration, knowledge, skill, relaxation, and broaden your perspective on life. When you are on a team and you have a coach or coaches, you should certainly listen to all they have to say about how to improve. However, if you want to learn from the greatest coaches of all time, they are only a library card away. If you want to have a conversation with the greatest who have ever played your sport, you only need to go to the bookstore. To get motivated, there are tons of inspirational books on how to better yourself. If you are an individual sport participant, there are countless books on how to teach yourself and become better. Often it is hard to find a very good golf, tennis, swimming, pole vaulting, etc., coach and thus the more you can read or watch videos on a topic the better off you will be.

If you have an overactive mind that needs to quiet down to help you rest and sleep, reading is a great choice. Reading books, and things closely related to it, such as watching instructional videos, reading magazines, surfing particular websites, is often a much better choice then all other forms of entertainment. The reason is that you can get very specific on what you want to study. When watching television, many programs are made for large groups of the population. But if you want to study the art of "Pass Blocking for Tight Ends," there are many articles, books, internet sites, and videos that you can find. Be selective with what you allow to enter into your brain.

95.
Affirmations

"I will act now. I will act now. I will act now. Henceforth, I will repeat these words each hour, each day, everyday, until the words become as much a habit as my breathing, and the action which follows becomes as instinctive as the blinking of my eyelids. With these words I can condition my mind to perform every action necessary for my success. I will act now. I will repeat these words again and again and again. I will walk where failures fear to walk. I will work when failures seek rest. I will act now for now is all I have. Tomorrow is the day reserved for the labor of the lazy. I am not lazy. Tomorrow is the day when the failure will succeed. I am not a failure. I will act now. Success will not wait. If I delay, success will become wed to another and lost to me forever. This is the time. This is the place. I am the person."
\- Og Mandino

You will eventually become what you think. Food fuels your body and thoughts fuel your mind. Just as you can control what you put in your mouth, you can control what you put in your mind. Affirmations are simply phrases that when repeated on a regular basis can alter the way you think, and therefore, behave. You need to write them down and repeat them several times a day. You can use one of them for several weeks or use ten for a few months. Whatever works for you. Here are some examples.

"I will wake up every morning and start the day off peacefully. I will calm my mind through breathing and then eat a healthy breakfast."

"I will not react negatively to the adversity around me. When my teammates make a mistake or my coach sends in the wrong play, I will simply make the best of it."

"I will succeed. I have within me everything I need to achieve all my goals if each day I make small steps to reach them."

It can be sport specific if you like.

"I will work fast, throw strikes, and keep the ball down."

"I will not focus on the pass rush, but see the receivers downfield."

96.
Effort

"There's no ceiling on effort!"
- Harvey C. Fruehauf

*"Nothing great will ever be achieved without great men,
and men are great only if they are determined to be so."*
- Charles De Gaulle

ABOVE ALL ELSE, EFFORT IS IN YOUR CONTROL. YOU CANNOT CONTROL ALMOST ANYTHING ELSE IN YOUR LIFE BUT YOUR EFFORT. REGARDLESS OF YOUR SITUATION, YOUR POSITION IN LIFE, ON THE TEAM, ON THE JOB, AT HOME, FINANCIALLY, YOUR EFFORT IS THE MOST IMPORTANT THING. YOU WILL SET THE TONE FOR EVERY SQUARE INCH OF YOUR LIFE BY GIVING EVERYTHING YOU HAVE IN YOUR ATHLETIC CAREER. IT WILL SPILL OVER TO YOUR ACADEMIC LIFE, YOUR CAREER, YOUR HOME LIFE, EVERYTHING THAT MATTERS TO YOU. EFFORT, EFFORT, EFFORT. EFFORT IS UNDER YOUR CONTROL. YOU CAN BE LAST IN THE

RACE, BUT IF YOU RAN YOUR BEST RACE, YOU WON. IF YOU WON THE RACE BUT RAN AT HALF EFFORT, YOU LOST. YOU ARE ACCOUNTABLE TO YOURSELF. LOOK IN THE MIRROR AND YOU WILL KNOW ABOUT YOUR EFFORT.

97.
What Are Your Priorities?

"The key is not to prioritize what's on your schedule,
but to schedule your priorities."
- Stephen R. Covey

You can do just about anything you want in the world. However, you cannot do everything you want in the world. If you are a college student for example, playing at a high NCAA level, then you have a great deal of responsibility. You have practice, workouts, study hall, games, travel, film study, and a list that goes on and on. This commitment, coupled with all your academic work and your social life will fill your plate. If you then try to add in having a job, playing a second sport, writing for the school paper, being in the theater group, at some point you will have way to many masters. If you try to serve them all, soon you will not serve any. As they say, you will become a jack-of-all-trades and master of none.

It is certainly not up to others or me to determine what you should and should not focus on, but just know that you cannot do it all. When you spread yourself too thin, soon you will find that those who have committed themselves full time to one area will pass you. The actor who makes it his priority will soon be more talented then you. The point guard who spends all year working on her game will soon be better then you. While you should certainly be well rounded, just realize that to be great at anything in life, it takes focus. Figuring out what your priorities are will help you determine where your time should be spent and also help you when you need to make a decision on what to do. If you play football and there is also a play you want to be in, but it is during the football season, and football is higher on your list, you play football and forget the theater. If the play is in the spring and you can fit it into your schedule, by all means audition and perform if you make it.

Obviously your family should come first. If there is a practice or game to be played and there is trouble at home, that should be an easy choice. For the majority of you, schoolwork or career will be next on the list. If you are serious about your sport, that might come next. I have seen many athletes be very committed to their sport then start a relationship and they no longer treat the sport as they once did. Then the relationship fizzles and they are back giving a full-time commitment. This is not to say that you cannot have a great relationship and be an athlete, but realize that if you are focused the relationship will add to your life and involvement in sports, not take away from it. Maybe you decide to workout with your new partner or teach them your sport. But to stop working as hard because you are in the excitement of a new relationship will be something you regret if it does not work out and your athletic careers suffers as a consequence.

98.
Details

"Excellence is in the details. Give attention to the details and excellence will come."
- Perry Paxton

For the majority of athletics, the highest achievers are those that tend to the details. In baseball, it's one thing to have a good arm and another to be a complete pitcher. The complete pitcher is one who has good stuff but also has great location on his pitches, knows all the bunt plays, pick offs, and first and third plays. He fields his position well, holds runners close, and keeps his composure. A quarterback who knows the details, opponents defensive schemes, the responsibilities of all the players on his team, will soon find success. If he does not pay attention to these things, it will soon be evident when he throws interceptions because he does not know exactly where his team or opponent is supposed to be. Each sport will have similar examples. Details are often the dirty work, they might seem less rewarding on the outside, but are crucial to your performance.

Those of you who work know very well that those who handle the details on the job are those that move ahead the quickest. If you are in charge of an event and don't plan ahead for all the details, you will be in trouble. Let's say the event is a fundraising dinner for a corporation. Here might be all the things you need to consider. When is the event? Does the date and time conflict with holidays, other events, weather, traffic, etc.? Does the location work for the majority of those who are coming? Is there sufficient parking? Have you sent out the invites at the right time? Did you follow up on the invites? How do you track those who have signed up? Payment information. Food order? What did you pay for the printing of the invites? The food? The hotel or restaurant where it will be held?

How will you determine seating? What if someone does not care for the prepared food? Vegetarians? Is the audio and video system in place? What if a speaker is not available at the last minute? If there is a major snowstorm how will you cancel? When will you reschedule? Will you give prizes at the door? Will you have the date for next year pick out so that you can give people time to book early for next year? Will you have feedback sheets for those that attended to better the event? Will you notify those that did not attend what they missed out on to create desire for the future? Will you do advertising or promotion for the event? I could go on and on. Not every sport or job has this kind of detail, but most have some form of it. Become the kind of person who looks after the little things and this will soon lead to much bigger and better things to come.

99.
Sunrise/Set

"Climb up on some hill at sunrise. Everybody needs perspective once in a while, and you'll find it there."
- Robb Sagendorph

As with each suggestion in this book, it may or may not work for you. Take what works for you, tweak it, and make the best of it. This one certainly works for me. I find that I am tremendously creative, motivated, and inspired at sunrise and sunset. Regardless of where you are, seeing a sunrise or set always seems to be peaceful. It puts the hustle and bustle of life on hold. It brings the sun closer to your heart and soul and seems to make the world suddenly not seem so large. Watching from the roof of a building in the city, or the beach, from a field, top of a mountain, or by a lake the sun turning orange and red and reflecting off the clouds is an amazing experience. While both are so beautiful it seems silly to compare, I prefer the sunrise. The sunrise usually happens when the majority of the world is still asleep. There is more little rush our traffic off in the distance, very little going on in the world. Sunrise takes work. It takes effort to get up in time to see it happen. Sunset, for most people, just happens during the day, it did not take any special effort to achieve. I often time my walks or jogs with my dog on the beach just before sunrise so that in the middle of my outing the sun will rise just over the water and warm and inspire me.

If you wish to find answers to issues, clear your head, or simply just relax, finding a peaceful way to really enjoy the rise or setting of the sun is one of the best things you can do.

100.
Don't Save It All For The End

"You don't save a pitcher for tomorrow. Tomorrow it may rain."
- Leo Durocher

You see it in every sport. Basketball teams that play their hearts out for the last two minutes. Football teams that go to the hurry up at games end. Baseball teams that make noise in the dugout during the last inning. While it is human nature to give it your all at the end, it is a fact that if you wait until the end to give your best effort, then the end won't often matter. This happens a lot for casual runners who run in road races. Since they are not experienced runners, they run the whole race at a much slower pace and then sprint at the end, where as the more experienced runner will run harder the entire time since they know how to pace themselves. A boxer should of course fight his or heart out in the last round, but often if they save energy just for the last round, they may not make it there or win the fight. Sometimes, when you save it all up for the end, the end is not worth saving up for.

101.
Think, Think, Think, Then Don't

"The life which is unexamined is not worth living."
-Plato

In sports, music, acting and any other performance endeavor, what it takes to prepare often requires us to think a great deal. An actor must learn her craft, how to move, how to emote, the lines to speak. This takes a great deal of practice and thinking to get to the level where one is ready to perform for an audience. But when that time comes, all the thinking and rehearsing, all the dedication to prepare, should lead to a performance where one just is. You simply perform. You are in the moment and all the practice leads you to be able not to think, but just to be the character. Imagine a musician who has to constantly think of what note to play. For the athlete, if you are thinking of mechanics in the game, or thinking of the play to run, you are in trouble. Almost all athletes will talk about peak performance as a time when they were just in the moment and almost turned off their mind because things occurred so naturally.

I am sure we can all remember when we learned to drive, especially if it was a standard car. I can recall thinking so much when learning to drive, that I was a danger on the road. Now after enough practice, I drive so automatically, that I never think about it. Many such examples apply.

Any time you want to pursue excellence, you must use your mind in a way that requires a great deal of thinking. But when it is time to achieve excellence, just let it go and be.

Twelve Things To Remember:

1. The value of time.
2. The success of perseverance.
3. The pleasure of working.
4. The dignity of simplicity.
5. The worth of character.
6. The power of kindness.
7. The influence of example.
8. The obligation of duty.
9. The wisdom of economy.
10. The virtue of patience.
11. The improvement of talent.
12. The joy of originating.

- Anonymous

$14.95 (1 copy)
$12.95 (2-10 copies)
$10.95 (11-20 copies)
$8.95 (20+ copies)

For additional copies of **You vs. You: Sports Psychology for Life**
please visit **www.mazzmarketing** or email **wmazz22@aol.com**.

Also by Wayne Mazzoni:
The Athletic Recruiting & Scholarship Guide
The Athletes Instruction Book
The Left-Handed Pick-Off Move